WEATHER AT SEA

WEATHER AT SEA

David Houghton

Fernhurst Books

First published in 1986 by
Fernhurst Books, Duke's Path, High Street, Arundel,
West Sussex, BN18 9AJ, England

New Edition 1991

Printed and bound in Great Britain

British Library Cataloguing in Publication Data
Houghton, David 1928
    Weather at sea.—2nd. ed.
    1. Oceans. Weather. Forecasting
    I. Title II. Series
    551.630247971

    ISBN 0-906754-64-X

Acknowledgements
Thanks are due to Bill Anderson of the RYA for his
helpful comments on the manuscript.

The publishers gratefully acknowledge permission
to reproduce the following photographs:
Tim Davison: page 47.
John Driscoll: cover.
Tim Hore: page 42.
Mike Peyton: 59, 66.
R. K. Pilsbury, FRPS: pages 28, 29, 30, 32, 33.
State University of New York: page 35.
University of Dundee: pages 8, 13, 20, 21, 45, 53.
Yachting Monthly: page 65.
Yachting Photographics: 22, 49, 63, 64.

Composition by Central Southern Typesetters, Hove
Printed by Hollen Street Press, Berwick upon Tweed

Contents

1 Weather basics

When we talk about weather we mean everything going on in the atmosphere around us: its temperature, which affects our comfort; its humidity, which determines how far we can see through it; its cloudiness and whether it is raining; and in particular the speed and direction in which it is moving, which determines where and how fast we can sail.

Apart from the air itself, there are three fundamental components of our weather: heat, water vapour and the rotation of the earth.

HEAT

Heat from the sun is the energy which drives all the main wind systems around the world. It can be compared to a garden bonfire heating the air which rises, carrying smoke with it, to be replaced by colder air moving in around the sides (figure 1.1). On the world scale, we have hot air rising over equatorial areas being replaced by cold air moving in from the polar regions; and on a local scale we have sea breezes, for example, when air warmed over land that is heated by the sun rises to be replaced by colder air moving in from the sea.

The world's wind systems are quite complicated for two reasons. One reason is the very uneven distribution around the world of land and sea, mountains and valleys, deserts and forests, and so on, which means that some areas become much hotter than others, even in similar latitudes. Another reason is the deflecting force, known as the Coriolis force, created by the rotation of the earth about its axis. This force depends on the latitude: the higher the latitude, the stronger it is. The structure of the major wind systems over the oceans is largely a consequence of Coriolis force, an example being the change from steady trade winds in low latitudes to disturbed westerlies in higher latitudes as the Force increases. The major wind systems over the oceans are shown in figure 1.2.

WATER VAPOUR

Water vapour is responsible for cloud and fog: suspensions in the air of millions of tiny water droplets or ice crystals. More importantly, it is responsible for much of the active weather we experience

Figure 1.2

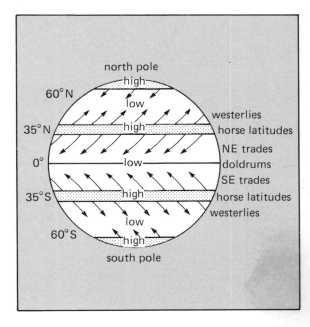

Figure 1.1

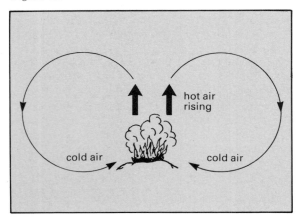

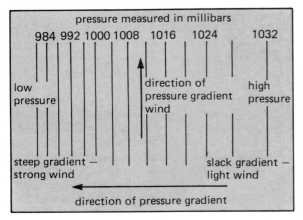

Figure 1.3 – Relationship between horizontal pressure gradient and wind.

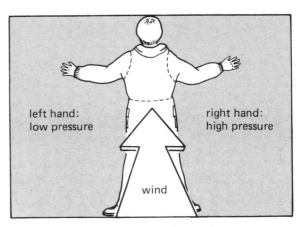

Figure 1.4 – Illustration of Buys Ballot's law.

because it moves heat energy around. Water is continually evaporating from oceans, lakes and moist ground, and this evaporation absorbs heat energy (latent heat). If you hold a wet finger in the wind it will feel cold because the process of vaporising the water takes heat out of your finger. Once the water vapour is in the air it moves around the world, and wherever it condenses into water droplets the same amount of heat energy that was used in evaporation is released back into the atmosphere. Tropical cyclones and thunderstorms derive much of their energy directly from this source – that is from the release of heat by condensation of the water vapour – so it really is very important. In fact, wherever you have rain you are likely to find stronger winds because of the extra energy available from the release of latent heat – along fronts and troughs of low pressure, for instance, as we will see later.

THE ROTATION OF THE EARTH

The easiest and traditional way to map the winds of the world is to map the weight or pressure of the atmosphere at the earth's surface. I say 'traditional' because nowadays we have satellite pictures which reveal the clouds acting like dye in the air to map out the large-scale wind systems. The benefit of using the pressure pattern is that there is a direct relationship between the difference in pressure between two points (the pressure gradient) and the wind. Wherever there is a pressure gradient there is a wind whose strength is proportional to the gradient.

If the earth did not rotate the wind would blow directly from high pressure to low pressure, as you would expect. But the Coriolis force always achieves a balance with the pressure gradient force and makes the wind blow across the pressure gradient (except near the equator).

There is no need to understand Coriolis force to appreciate and interpret a weather map. All you need to know is that, except near the equator, the wind blows across the pressure gradient with a strength which is proportional to it (figure 1.3). If you want a full explanation you will find it in Appendix 1, but the following simple illustration will start you thinking on the right lines. Imagine a golf ball driven from, say, London to Paris. As the ball moves southeast the ground beneath it will be moving eastwards at an increasing speed, since the nearer you get to the equator the more ground there is to spin through in 24 hours. So although the golf ball maintains its initial eastward ground speed it will be left behind and appear to drift westwards.

The trade winds are a good example of the Coriolis effect. Air moving south towards the equator appears to be deflected to the west, giving us the Northeast Trades. Northward moving air in the southern hemisphere is also deflected to the west, giving us the Southeast Trades. The Coriolis force disappears near the equator and is ineffective between about 8 degrees north and 8 degrees south. Tropical storms which need the Coriolis force to start them spinning never form in these lowest latitudes.

The direction of the wind deflection due to the Coriolis force is best remembered by Buys Ballot's Law which says that if you stand with your back to the wind in the northern hemisphere you will have low pressure on your left-hand side (figure 1.4). The opposite applies south of the equator.

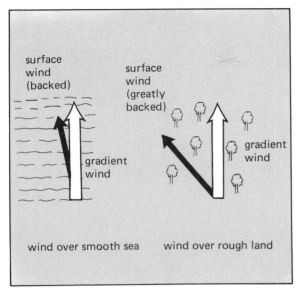

Figure 1.5

The wind created by the pressure gradient is the wind you measure on your weather map. Meteorologists, recognising the importance of the Coriolis force, call it the geostrophic (earth turning) wind. We will use the simpler name 'pressure gradient wind'.

The pressure gradient wind is the wind experienced at a height of about 500 metres above the ground: sufficiently high not to be influenced by friction and land/sea effects. It is a real wind and wherever there are low clouds you can observe it. Make a point of doing so because when you are on land or in harbour it is the best guide you have to the wind over the nearest sea.

It stands to reason that closely spaced isobars indicating a strong pressure gradient mean strong winds, and widely spaced isobars indicating a weak pressure gradient mean light winds. If you are sailing far afield it is important to realise that the latitude comes into the equation as well, since it affects the Coriolis force. The lower the latitude the stronger the wind for the same spacing of the isobars.

Opposite: Satellite picture showing cumulus clouds of varying sizes over relatively warm land, some arranged in rows. Wind WNW.

THE SURFACE WIND

The surface wind is what you actually experience at the surface, on land or sea. It is not quite the same as the wind at low cloud level because friction prevents an exact balance between the pressure gradient and Coriolis force. As a result the wind near the surface is slowed down and blows at an angle across the isobars towards low pressure. The greater the friction, the more it is slowed and the larger the angle.

Over the sea the surface wind is normally about 15 degrees backed from the gradient wind and about 15 to 30 per cent lighter. Over land the difference is some 30 to 40 degrees in direction and as much as 50 per cent or more in strength (figure 1.5).

STABILITY AND INSTABILITY

Another factor which influences the surface wind is the stability of the air: the ease with which the air aloft can get down to the surface, bringing its wind with it to replace the air which has been slowed by friction.

The words stable and unstable are used to describe how buoyant the air is, that is how easily it rises. Air that is warmed, for instance when the land surface is heated by the sun, becomes buoyant (unstable) and rises. Air which is cooled, often at night

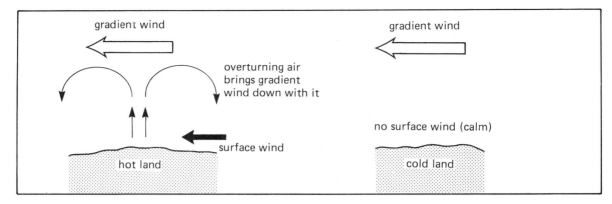

Figure 1.6

over cold ground, becomes stable and resists any attempt to make it turn over. Unstable air is continually overturning so that the wind aloft is brought down to the surface in gusts. In stable air there is little inter-action with the air higher up so the air near the ground may stop moving altogether (figure 1.6).

An air mass (see below) is described as unstable when only a small amount of heating at the earth's surface causes the air to rise to considerable heights.

Over land there is a 24-hour cycle in the stability of the air which is responsible for a very marked 24-hour cycle in wind strength (figure 1.7). The sun heats the ground and thus the air near it. This air becomes increasingly unstable and as it rises and is replaced by colder air from aloft the wind increases because the air aloft is moving with the pressure gradient wind. As the sun goes down the temperature falls and the wind decreases. After dusk, if there is little or no cloud, the ground cools rapidly and then cools the air near it making it stable, so the wind quickly dies away.

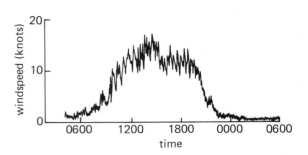

Figure 1.7 – Typical diurnal variation of windspeed over land on a sunny day.

A variation in wind through the day may also occur at sea, but it is often masked by other events such as a change in water temperature. The water tempera-ture is likely to change as the tide changes, and near estuaries the river water must be expected to have a different temperature to the sea. The consequent variations in wind can be important, particularly if you are looking for wind (see Chapter 14).

Figure 1.8

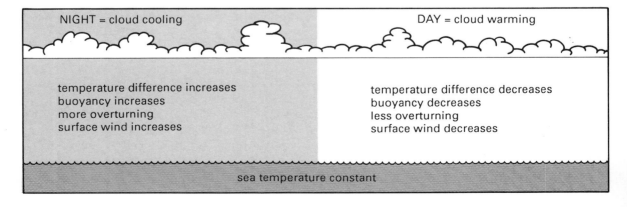

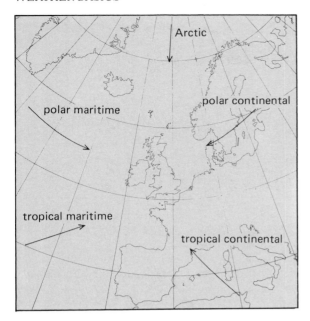

Figure 1.9 – Air masses affecting northwest Europe.

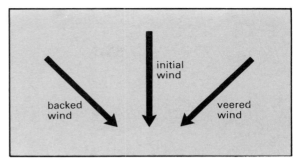

Figure 1.10

One easily understood, yet commonly overlooked influence on the wind at sea is the varying temperature at the top of low cloud. If the low cloud persists day and night the sea temperature will stay constant – there is no sun to warm it, and no clear sky to allow it to cool – but the top of the cloud will warm up by day and cool down at night (figure 1.8). The colder the cloud top and the greater the temperature drop with height, the more unstable the air and the stronger the wind. The warmer the cloud top and the smaller the temperature drop with height, the more stable the air and the lighter the wind. Hence under a cloudy sky, the wind will be strongest in the early hours and lightest in the afternoon – so long as the pressure gradient is not changing.

AIR MASSES

An air mass is simply a large volume of air of fairly uniform character. Air masses are named according to where they come from: 'Arctic', 'polar', 'tropical' and so on. If they originate over a continent they are 'continental' and if they come from over the sea they are 'maritime'. The names may be linked to give more precise descriptions, such as 'polar continental' and 'tropical maritime'. Their origin determines their character – air from a continent is dry and air from over the sea is relatively wet, and I hardly need add that tropical air is warm and Arctic air is cold. The air masses affecting north-west Europe are shown in figure 1.9.

BACKING AND VEERING

When there is a change in the direction in which the wind is blowing, the wind is said to *veer* if it swings in a clockwise direction, and to *back* if it swings in an anticlockwise direction. This is illustrated in figure 1.10.

2 Weather systems

We have noticed from satellite pictures how the clouds map out some of the movements of the atmosphere. If you could actually see the air itself from the satellite, if it was instantaneously 'frozen' and the clouds removed, you would see a whole landscape of mountains and hollows, ridges, valleys and cols all over the globe, overlaid by something looking like two or three vast meandering rivers, in places narrow and obviously flowing very fast, the main ones centered in mid-latitudes. 'Unfreeze' the air and let it move again and you would see the air in the hollows and mountains circulating around the centres: hence the names *cyclone* and *anticyclone*, the two circulations being in opposite directions. In the northern hemisphere this circulation is anti-clockwise around the low (cyclone) and clockwise around the high (anticyclone). In a newly formed depression this spiralling motion is shallow, extending upwards only a thousand metres or so, and it moves downstream, steered by the 'river' of air overlying it. In an older depression the depth of the spiral may be 10,000 to 15,000 metres and the 'river' will be seen meandering around it. There is a direct similarity between a contour map of the earth's surface with its lines of equal height, and a weather map with its lines of equal pressure (*isobars*). The mountains are called *highs* and the hollows *lows*, the valleys *troughs*, and the *ridges* and *cols* keep the same names (figure 2.1).

If you were able to fill the air with a tracer dye which enabled you to study its movements not only horizontally but also vertically, you would see a very gradual descent of air in the high-pressure areas and a slightly faster and somewhat uneven ascent of air in the low-pressure areas. It is this ascent and descent of air which really makes 'weather' – the variety of rain, cloud, sunshine and showers, changing from day to day and week to week. Rising air cools, and as it cools cloud forms and then rain falls. Conversely, descending (or subsiding) air warms, the cloud disperses and we have fine weather.

Now we can understand the different sorts of weather we have in ridges and troughs. Ridges have the same character as anticyclones with gradually subsiding air and fine weather, while troughs are characterised by rising air, cloud and rain. In fact the ascent of air in a depression is often concentrated along the troughs; hence they are bands of thicker cloud and heavier rain with relatively bright weather either side. The heat energy which is released as the rain falls contributes to stronger winds in troughs. Incidentally the rate of movement of air up and down in lows and highs is so slow it is virtually impossible to measure it directly. It amounts to a few metres a day – very different from the much more rapid upward motion found in cumulus and particularly in cumulonimbus clouds, where rising air currents at speeds of 60 knots have been encountered.

Figure 2.1

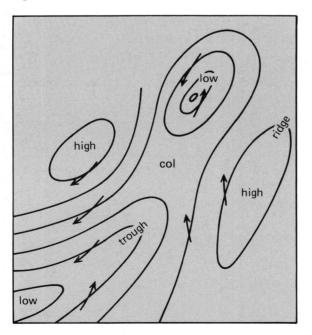

Right: Britain enjoying a mainly sunny afternoon in a weak ridge of high pressure between the clouds of a small, shallow depression over the North Sea, and a deepening low approaching from the west. Time 1524 on 31 August 1988. See overleaf for the weather map three hours earlier.

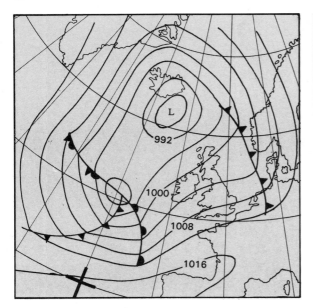 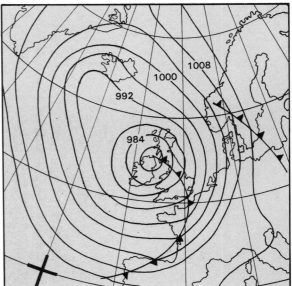

Figures 2.2 and 2.3: The weather map for 1200 GMT on 31 August 1988, and (right) the weather map for 24 hours later (see page 45).

One particular sort of trough is a front, a boundary between air masses of different characteristics. In many shipping bulletins it may simply be called a trough. A front will only be found in a trough of low pressure but the majority of troughs are not fronts. The special characteristics of a front are easy to understand and the sequence of cloud of different types is fascinating to follow as a front passes by.

Textbooks on meteorology often give a lot of space to fronts but they are relatively rare events. One month several may pass, sometimes one or two months will go by without a single sighting.

3 The life of a depression

We now have an idea of how, within the earth's atmosphere, depressions and anticyclones are continually developing and dying. Some last only a day or two; some, particularly the larger anticyclones, last for weeks on end. Some move quickly – they are the relatively shallow systems steered by the fast-flowing river of air in mid-latitudes. Some remain virtually stationary, particularly the larger anticyclones. There is an infinite variety. No two weather systems are ever identical. So in describing them we must be content with describing typical features and behaviour.

It is a bit like observing a river of water from the bank. There is the main flow, normally (but not always) near the centre, while eddies in the flow are continually developing and then dying as they are carried away downstream. Most of the eddies form near the banks or where rocks interrupt the flow; just as in the earth's atmosphere most eddies form near the surface or to the lee of mountains.

The energy needed for the eddies in the river of water comes from the energy of the main flow as the water runs downhill. Energy to drive the eddies in the atmosphere comes both from the main flow and from local sources of heat, particularly latent heat. In temperate latitudes depressions are more likely to develop where warm and cold air masses meet, especially if there is plenty of moisture as well: if one of the air masses is tropical maritime, for instance.

Typically, depressions affecting Western Europe develop over the Atlantic where cold polar air meets warm tropical air, and then move eastwards steered by the river of air aloft. This boundary between the warm and cold air is known as the polar front (figure 3.1). There is always much cloud near it since the relatively buoyant warm air likes to rise over the denser cold air, and indeed the cold air likes to push its nose under the warm air and lift it off the ground. If the boundary is moving so that warm air is displacing cold air it is called a warm front. If it is moving the other way, so that cold air is displacing warm, it is called a cold front.

In short, there is warm air behind a warm front and cold air behind a cold front.

We have already noted that the preferred situation for eddies to form in the atmosphere is near the earth's surface, subject to there being plenty of energy available. The first sign of a new depression is normally a wobble in the surface wind blowing near the polar front (figure 3.2).

Figure 3.1

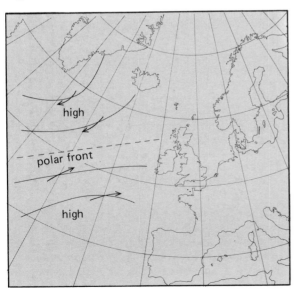

Figure 3.2

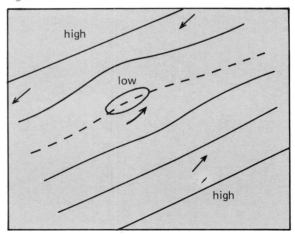

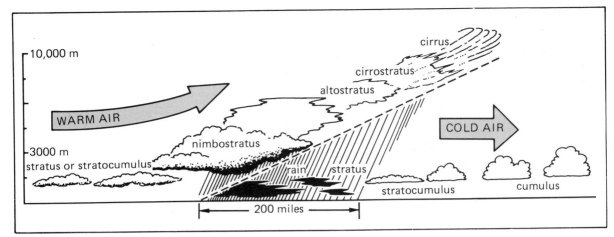

Figure 3.3 – Vertical section through a typical warm front.

Simultaneously the satellite picture will reveal thicker cloud, which speaks of latent heat being released and more energy becoming available for the cyclonic circulation to develop. As the new low develops a recognisable circulation it increasingly distorts the boundary between the cold and warm air masses (figure 3.4), and within a matter of hours we have an advancing boundary of warm air – the warm front – ahead of the new low, and an advancing boundary of cold air behind it – the cold front – each with its typical cloud formation (figures 3.3, 3.5, 3.6).

It must be emphasised that while it is useful to identify and describe typical cloud formations and sequences associated with warm and cold fronts, they are only typical. Just as no two depressions are ever identical so are no two fronts ever identical.

As the low develops the warm air will increasingly rise over the cold air ahead of it, and the cold air to the rear will increasingly undercut the warm air, in each case giving more cloud, more rain, and more energy to help drive the strengthening winds. The typical catalogue of events is as follows.

Day 1
The pressure falls, particularly along the fronts and in the region of the centre. Hence the pressure gradient increases and the wind strengthens. It is important to note that by simple geometry deep

Figure 3.5

Figure 3.4

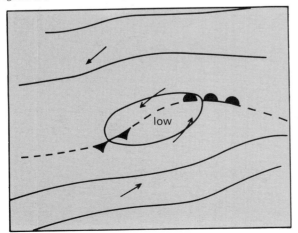

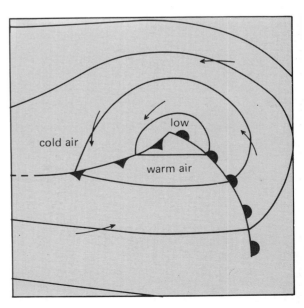

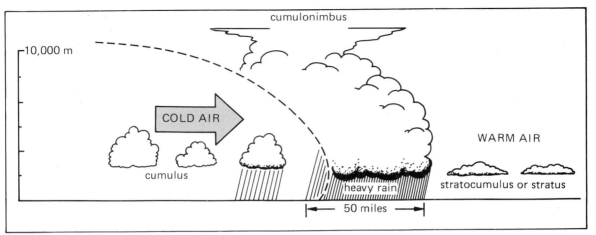

Figure 3.6 – Vertical section through a typical vigorous cold front.

troughs will always have stronger pressure gradients and therefore stronger winds than shallow troughs of low pressure.

The new low moves in the direction of the wind above it and may achieve speeds of 60 knots or more depending on the strength of this wind (figure 3.7).

Days 2–3
The distortion of the surface wind field extends steadily upwards. As the upper wind field becomes distorted the depression slows down, and typically

turns to the left – but this depends on what the upper wind direction was to start with.

At the surface, since for a given pressure gradient the cold air moves faster than the warm air, the cold air behind the cold front gradually pushes the warm air upwards and out of the way.

The cold front thus catches up with the warm front and we are left at the surface with an occluded front or occlusion (figure 3.8). The vertical slope of this occlusion will depend on whether the cold air behind the cold front is colder or warmer than the cold air

Figure 3.7

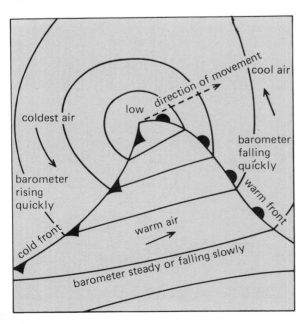

Figure 3.8

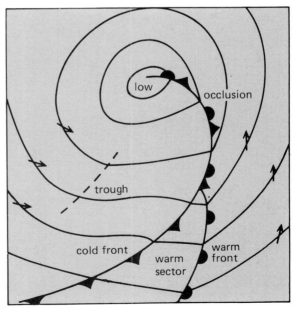

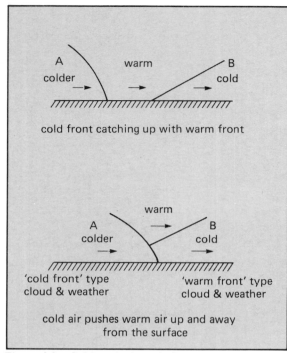

Figure 3.9 – Cold occlusion: air A colder than air B.

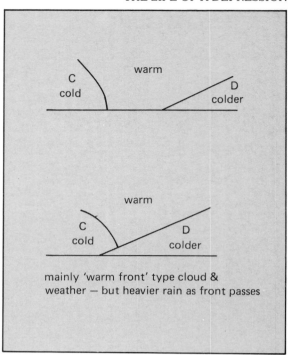

Figure 3.10 – Warm occlusion: air C less cold than air D.

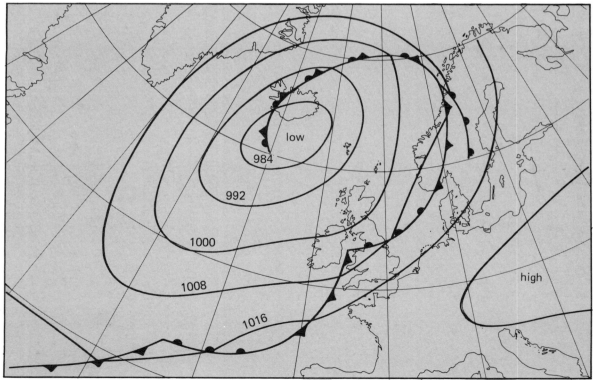

Figure 3.11 – Large, old occluded depression with waves on cold front.

Typical sequence of weather associated with a cold front

	Front approaching	As it passes	In cold air behind it
Wind	backs & increases close to front	sudden veer often with squall	probably backs a little then direction steady; stronger & gusty
Cloud	stratus & stratocumulus thickening to nimbostratus	cumulonimbus	often total clearance; cumulus develops
Rain	heavy rain near front	heavy rain, perhaps hail & thunder	usually fine for an hour or two, then showers
Visibility	moderate or poor, perhaps fog	poor in rain	very good
Pressure	falls near front	sudden rise	rise gradually levels off
Dewpoint	little change	sudden fall	little change

Typical sequence of weather associated with a warm front

	Front approaching	As it passes	In warm sector
Wind	increases & backs	veers	direction steady
Cloud	sequence of cirrus, cirrostratus, altostratus, nimbostratus, stratus	nimbostratus	stratus, stratocumulus
Rain	becomes heavier & more continuous	stops or turns to drizzle	occasional drizzle or light rain
Visibility	deteriorates slowly as rain gets heavier	deteriorates	moderate or poor; fog likely
Pressure	falls at increasing rate	stops falling	falls if depression deepening, otherwise steady
Dewpoint	little change	rises	little change

originally ahead of the warm front (figures 3.9, 3.10).

The main troughs of the depression will continue to coincide with the fronts, but subsidiary troughs of low pressure will develop, particularly in the cold air on its left-hand side. These will be characterised by bands of thicker cloud and probably showers. Between the subsidiary troughs minor ridges may appear, characterised by mainly clear skies.

Days 3–6

After three to four days of growth and development the depression will be large and slow-moving, with its centre usually somewhere between Iceland and Norway. Figure 3.11 is a typical example centred south of Iceland.

The fronts will become increasingly twisted around the centre and the cold front will trail away to the south-west or west, slotting into a trough which becomes shallower as you move away towards higher pressure. Typically the next stage is for a small wave depression to form on this cold front – which is still the polar front – usually between 300 and 500 miles from the centre of the parent low. It starts life just as the parent low did but frequently runs into the parent low and merges with it.

Sometimes the new wave depression will deepen even more than the parent low, and take up a position to the south or south-east of the original centre.

WHERE DEPRESSIONS FORM

Some 60 per cent of depressions develop on the polar front and evolve as I have just described. An actual sequence with corresponding weather maps and satellite pictures is shown overleaf. This is only one example. Some move and deepen very quickly, some slowly. Some have sharply defined cloud patterns, some very diffuse ones. Of the 40 per cent of depressions which form other than on the polar front the most common in western Europe are:

● In the lee of mountains – lee lows.
● In cold air moving over warm sea – polar lows.
● Over hot land areas in summer – heat lows.

An average weather map, for a month, for instance will show the most likely positions of low pressure and high pressure, and is useful for planning a voyage. But do not forget that it comprises a variety of day-to-day developments and movements of weather systems.

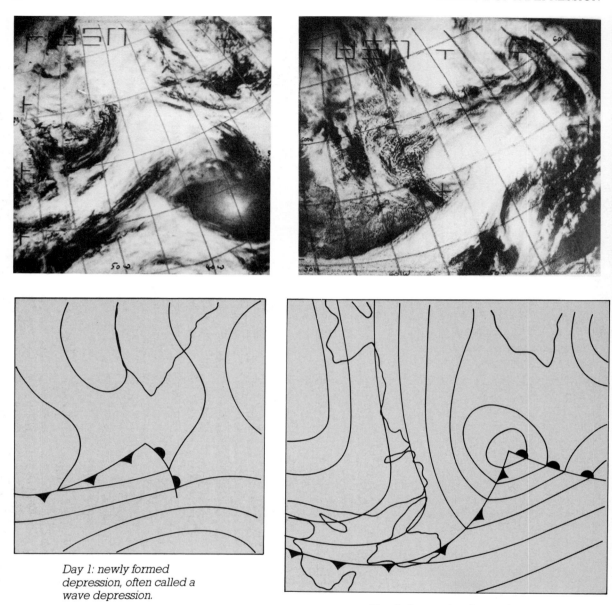

Day 1: newly formed
depression, often called a
wave depression.

Day 2: depression deepening
rapidly.

THE LIFE OF A DEPRESSION

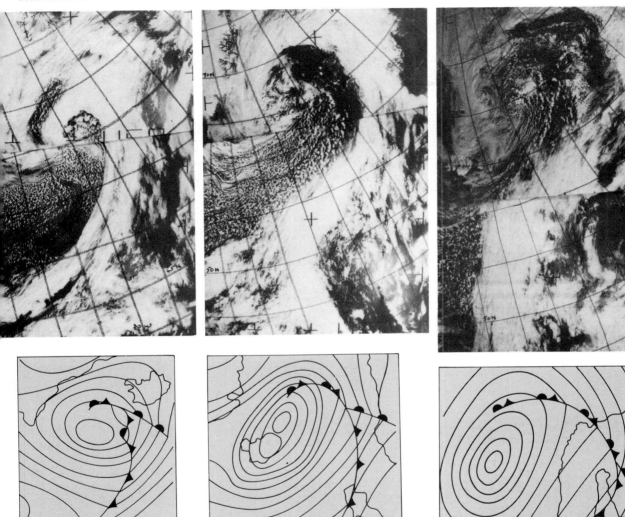

Day 3: depression occluding with a minor wave on the cold front running quickly into the centre.

Day 4: occlusion continues; signs of a major wave on the cold front.

Day 5: occluded mature depression. Old centre decaying; major wave developing on cold front.

4 Winds aloft and wind shear

We have seen already how the world's wind systems are thermally driven, with the sun providing the heat energy. So there is clearly some relationship between temperature and wind. This is fairly obvious in, for example, sea and land breezes, but perhaps not quite so obvious in the difference between winds at the surface and winds aloft. On some days this difference is well marked; there may be a southerly wind at the ground, but high-level clouds rushing across from the northwest.

As a sailor you do not need to know the meteorological reasons for this change of wind with height – they are given in Appendix 2 for those who want an explanation – but it is useful to know what it can mean in terms of weather to come. There are two very simple rules:
• A wind veering with height means advancing warm air and normally deteriorating weather.
• A wind backing with height means advancing cold air, and normally improving weather.
The opposite applies in the Southern Hemisphere in both cases.

The best illustration of this can be seen in the case of warm and cold fronts. In figures 3.3 and 3.6 the broad open arrows indicate only the component of wind across the fronts. The high and middle level clouds in figure 3.3 will be moving in a direction that is well veered from the surface wind, typically from the northwest when the surface wind is southerly. The stronger the upper level wind and the more veered it is, the more vigorous the advancing warm front, so this is a useful predictor of the weather a few hours ahead. With a cold front (figure 3.6) the higher clouds are often obscured until the front has passed, when you can look back and see them moving from a direction that is well backed from the surface wind – typically from the south when the surface wind has veered to the west or northwest. The faster the higher clouds are moving, the colder and more showery the weather is likely to be.

Left: On a yacht with a tall rig the effect of wind shear with height can be quite pronounced.

WIND SHEAR UP THE MAST

As explained in Chapter 1, the earth exerts a drag on the wind so that the nearer you are to the surface of the land or sea the slower the wind and the more backed its direction. This variation is noticeable even between the top of the mast and deck level. The difference may be very little in unstable air – about five per cent in speed and one or two degrees in direction – but in stable air it may be very substantial – up to 300 per cent in speed and 20 to 30 degrees in direction.

Figure 4.1 illustrates what happens. The curves are based on actual measurements over water from a mast fixed in the water, and relate to the true wind. Differences in relative wind between the top and bottom of the mast may be larger and will depend on which tack you are sailing. So in stable air you may need a lot of twist in your sails, while in unstable air the leeches can be much straighter.

This wind shear largely accounts for what is known as 'weight of wind'. Variations in wind speed between the top and bottom of the mast can cause a difference of something like 50 per cent in the heeling moment on the boat for the same measured wind speed. In stable air there will appear to be more weight in the wind for a given wind speed measured across the deck. Conversely, if your wind reference is a mast-head anemometer, there will seem to be less weight in the wind than the measured wind speed would suggest.

Figure 4.1

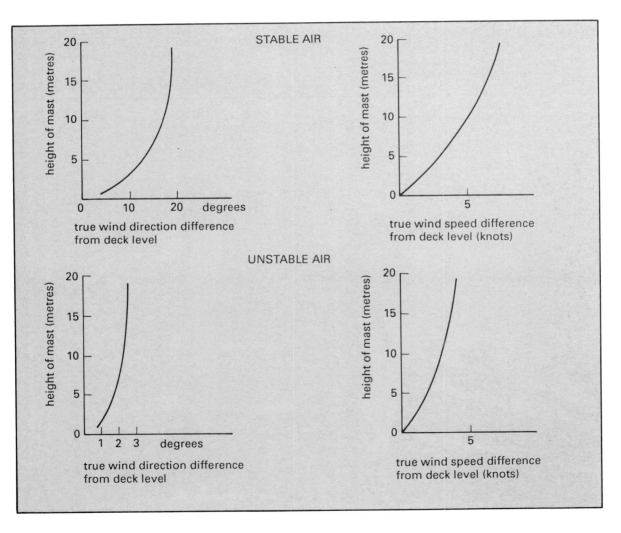

5 Moving weather

I am sometimes asked what happens to the wind in a depression when the depression itself is moving. If, for instance, a depression with 60-knot westerly winds south of the centre is moving east at 60 knots, what is the resultant wind? The answer is – 60 knots westerly. You see, depressions and anticyclones are like ripples in a pool. If you throw a stone into the pool the disturbance of the water moves outwards at a steady speed, but the water itself does not move outwards, only up and down through changes in pressure. Similarly in the atmosphere the movements of pressure systems are achieved by changes in pressure along their paths.

Let us look at some typical examples of what happens to the wind as weather systems pass by. We assume that you are moored in the open ocean, so there are no complications due to coastal effects and land or sea breezes. The sequence as a system passes by is usually similar to the sequence along a line passing through the system, modified by the changing orientation of troughs, ridges and fronts which rotate slowly anticlockwise around the centre.

A depression moves east to the north of you

AB is the track of a depression centre (figures 5.1, 5.2). As the depression moves towards B the fronts will be rotating around the centre, so while the sequence of wind speed and weather at your position X will be similar to that along the line XY the wind directions will be modified. The wind will increase and back, veer at the warm front, then steady in both speed and direction until it veers again at the cold front. The veer at the cold front (about 70 degrees in this example) is followed by a gradual back in direction and slackening in speed as the ridge axis approaches.

A depression moves east to the south of you

AB is the track of another depression centre (figures 5.3, 5.4). It is moving east but this time to the south of

Figure 5.1

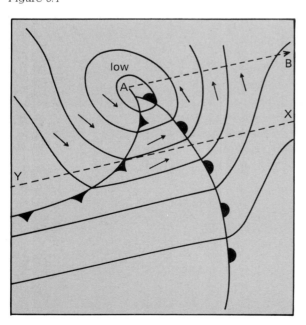

Figure 5.2 – Changes observed at point X as the depression in figure 5.1 moves from A to B.

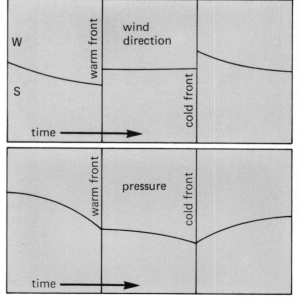

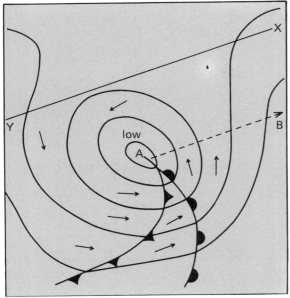

Figure 5.3

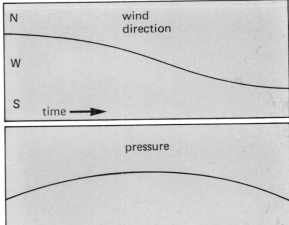

Figure 5.5

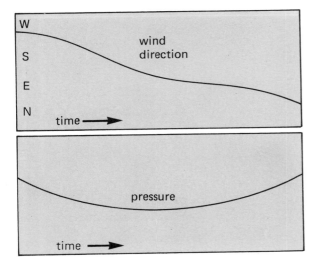

Figure 5.4 – Changes observed at point X as the depression in figure 5.3 moves from A to B.

Figure 5.6 – Changes observed at point X as the ridge in figure 5.5 moves across.

your position at X. There are no fronts along the line XY so sudden changes in wind speed and direction are unlikely. The wind just backs from WSW at the start through east to northerly at Y, perhaps modified by broad troughs circulating around the low centre.

A ridge moves across you

The ridge with axis H-H moves eastward (figure 5.5). The sequence to an observer at X will be as shown in figure 5.6, unless the ridge axis swings so that its orientation changes, in which case the sequence of wind directions will be modified. The wind will be steady at first, then gradually backing and decreasing as pressure rises to a maximum. Winds near the axis H-H will be very light, then they will increase again as the direction continues to back and the pressure falls.

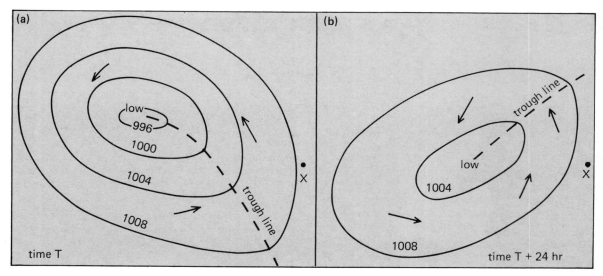

Figure 5.7

A stationary filling depression with a trough moving around it

The low centre remains in the same position relative to yours at X (figures 5.7, 5.8). To determine the sequence of changes we must interpolate the values of wind speed, wind direction and pressure throughout the 24 hours.

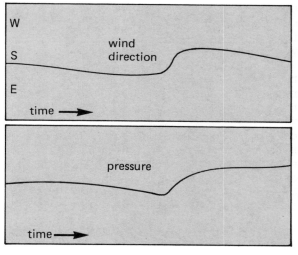

Figure 5.8 – Changes observed at point X over 24 hours.

6 The message of the clouds

Clouds show up a great variety of events in the atmosphere, some of them involving changes in the wind. On pictures taken from satellites above the earth, the clouds map out the large-scale weather systems, particularly the depressions with their attendant troughs and fronts, and suggest many and varied smaller-scale wind movements down to the limits of resolution of the pictures (about two miles).

Looked at from below, the clouds are just as meaningful. The sequence of clouds ahead of a typical warm front tells of the advance of the warm front and perhaps its depression as well (see chapter 3). But the majority of cloud messages relate to events on a much smaller scale, a mere few hundred metres or so. Cumulus clouds, for instance, tell of pockets of rising air which are replaced by air moving downwards in between the clouds.

Every cloud has a message of some sort, though not necessarily about the wind. The sailor needs to recognise features which relate to the character of the wind or to changes in the general weather picture which herald major changes in wind speed and direction. In general the message of the high clouds is about events far aloft or at least several hours ahead, while low clouds provide evidence of wind changes from minutes to two or three hours ahead. We must also try to rule out signs which are unimportant or capable of misleading.

COLOURED CLOUDS

The colour of a cloud depends on how it is illuminated. If the sun is shining on it the cloud will appear white; if the sun is behind it, it will appear dark. If it is illuminated at a glancing angle when the sun is rising or setting it will be beautifully coloured. The colour will change as the cloud moves across the sky or as the sun moves over the sky. This change in colour normally has no significance where the wind is concerned, except for that enshrined in the well-known adage 'red sky in the morning, shepherd's warning; red sky at night, shepherd's delight'. This saying is well founded. The most colourful skies at sunrise are when high clouds are increasing from the west and illuminated at a glancing angle by the sun – and we know that high clouds increasing from the west are characteristic of an advancing depression and bad weather to come. Conversely, clouds breaking up from the west are often the last evidence of a trough moving away to the east, and illuminated by the setting sun these too appear beautifully coloured. The bad weather has gone by, and is likely to be followed by a ridge of high pressure.

NAMES OF CLOUDS

Clouds are named and classified according to their height and shape (see photographs and figure 6.1). Flat clouds are defined by the word *stratus* (meaning 'layer') or the prefix *strato-*. Lumpy or heaped clouds are described by the word *cumulus* (meaning 'heap') or the prefix *cumulo-*. Feathery clouds high in the atmosphere are known as *cirrus* (meaning 'tuft' or 'curl') and the prefix *cirro-* is used to describe other clouds in the middle levels of the atmosphere. The words *stratus* and *cumulus* on their own identify

Figure 6.1

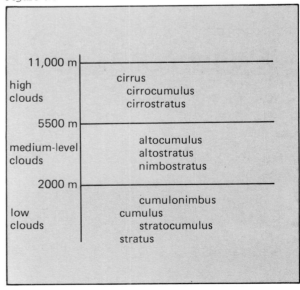

clouds whose base is below 2000 m. *Stratocumulus* is a layer of low cloud which has lumpy or roll features. *Nimbus* is used to describe a raining cloud. *Cumulus* may be combined with *nimbus* to give *cumulonimbus* – heaped rain cloud. A layer cloud from which rain is falling is *nimbostratus*.

FLAT CLOUDS

Flat clouds are characteristic of stable air. They often possess some shape or structure but this is usually due to warming or cooling of the top of the cloud and must not be interpreted in terms of any wind pattern at the surface. However a large and distinctive feature appearing in a layer of cloud may be significant.

A line or band of low cloud, or thicker cloud within a cloud layer, may indicate a change in wind speed or direction or both. If the line or band is stationary it may be due to local convergence of airstreams caused by a feature of the nearby land or a significant change in water temperature over the sea. If the line is moving it is clearly a feature of the air mass and a small windshift (normally a veer) is likely as it passes by. Think of these features in the atmosphere as small-scale replicas of the weather-map systems: an advancing line of cloud can be thought of as a very minor trough giving a small and probably temporary veer in the wind direction as it goes by.

If there is little or no wind an approaching line of stratocumulus cloud is likely to herald wind from a direction to the left of the line of advance; in other words the line of advance indicates the direction of an increasing gradient wind with the surface wind some 20 degrees to the left of it. However the approach of a bank of very low stratus or fog may herald less wind, because fog is often a feature of very stable air where vertical mixing is inhibited and the effect of friction becomes more pronounced. If the wind is light to start with the increased influence of friction on arrival of the fog may bring it to a complete halt.

There are very many variations on the theme of lines and bands of cloud, and it is important to realise that the atmosphere is never completely uniform over an area, even over a smooth sea. There are always variations and it is not easy, even for a meteorologist, to distinguish between those lines of cloud that suggest a wind change at the surface and those that do not.

Left, top: cirrus. Centre: cirrus increasing ahead of a warm front, cumulus below. Bottom: stratus.

Above: fair-weather cumulus. Below: a line of cumulus or 'cloud street'.

Large cumulus approaching cumulonimbus stage.

The top of this cumulus is flattening into stratocumulus –
typical of a ridge approaching.

Stratocumulus.

Altocumulus.

LUMPY CLOUDS

Lumpy or cumulus clouds are characteristic of unstable air. They are found most frequently over land in the afternoon when the temperature is at a maximum, when pockets of air heated at the ground rise until the cooling due to expansion brings their temperature back to that of the surrounding air.

Figure 6.2 – Formation of a cumulus cloud.

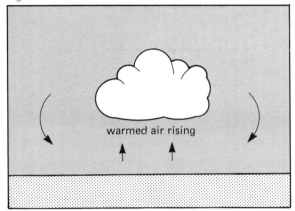

warmed air rising

Figure 6.3 – Cloud streets.

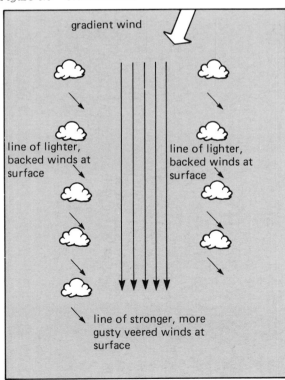

gradient wind

line of lighter, backed winds at surface

line of lighter, backed winds at surface

line of stronger, more gusty veered winds at surface

Look for a moment at a single cumulus cloud (figure 6.2). If it is stationary, that is if there is no gradient wind, air will rise from the heated surface into the cloud to be replaced by air moving down (subsiding) around the outside of the cloud, creating a very simple circulation pattern. The wind strength in the inflow area is indicated by the size of the cloud. For a small cloud, say 100 metres across and 300 metres in vertical extent, it will be less than a knot; but for a towering cumulus cloud of the order of 500 metres across and up to 5000 metres high it may be 15 or more knots.

In practice there is usually some pressure gradient wind, and the gentle convergence of air into a small cloud is only a very minor detail superimposed on the main wind.

CLOUD STREETS

Over the sea cumulus clouds are normally found in regularly spaced lines. The best examples of these are found in the trade winds where they extend for many tens of miles. Cloud streets show up a regular pattern in the vertical movement of air which is like a horizontal roll. Between the lines of cloud you will find the stronger, more gusty and slightly veered winds, and beneath the lines of cloud somewhat lighter and more backed winds (figure 6.3).

Sometimes near land you may notice a single cloud street, that is a single line of cumulus clouds downwind of something that is producing them – a hot spot, a hill or an island. Once produced, the cumulus clouds are carried away in a line stretching downwind for many miles and the pattern of lighter and backed wind under the street, and stronger and usually veered wind either side of it, will also persist.

RAINING CLOUDS

So far we have considered fair-weather clouds, or at least clouds where there is no sign of any rain falling. Rain makes a fundamental difference to the wind characteristics of a cumulus cloud. The main reason for this is that the first rain to fall out of the base of the cloud evaporates into the air beneath and cools it, often by several degrees. This cooled air descends and the more it is cooled the more rapidly it descends. Thus instead of air rising into a cloud we have not only rain falling out of the cloud, but air as well. The drier the air beneath the cloud the more it is capable of being cooled by evaporation, and so long as there

Cumulonimbus.

is enough rain coming out of the cloud the colder the air becomes. The cooled air will literally drop out from beneath the cloud with the rain and spread out in all directions at the surface. The light wind which was moving in towards the cloud suddenly becomes a squall rushing out and away from it (figure 6.4).

There is always plenty of visual evidence of this change. You can see the rain falling, often in grey streaks below the cloud, sometimes in a dramatic arch of black cloud spreading out from the parent cloud. The squall is necessarily short-lived because there is only a limited amount of air below the cloud to be cooled by evaporation of rain into it. Once the squall has passed the rain usually continues for a

while, some ten to twenty minutes for a typical shower cloud before it is exhausted. The wind coming out of the cloud will gradually die away with the rain.

The larger shower clouds, however, keep going for longer, and while rain falls from one part of the cloud, air continues to be drawn upwards into another part. The name 'cumulonimbus' is sometimes reserved for these big clouds. A large thunderstorm cumulonimbus may last for an hour or more – sometimes up to four hours.

Usually there is a pressure gradient wind, but often the squall from a reasonably sized shower cloud will temporarily override the pressure gradient wind, and will augment it where they are both in the same direction.

Figure 6.4 – Cooled air falling out of a raining cloud.

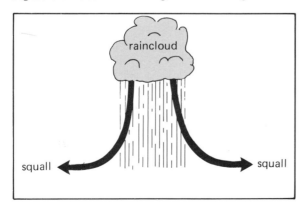

CLOUD BANDS

There are many different types of cloud band and they form for a wide variety of reasons. Most of them tell us something about the wind. Examples are bands of thicker (or thinner) cloud within a layer of cloud in stable air, lines of cumulus cloud, cloud streets and so on. A band of cloud may be observed lying along the coast, layered cloud if the air is stable or cumulus cloud if the air is unstable. If the coast is fairly flat this band is likely to indicate a convergence of airstreams. A hilly (and particularly a mountainous) coast will frequently appear cloudy simply because the air has

*Above: a band of high cloud – cirrocumulus and
altocumulus – a useful predictor of weather to come.
Right: castellated altocumulus often heralds thundery
weather.*

to rise over the high ground irrespective of wind
direction.

An approaching band of towering cumulus clouds
is usually associated with a trough of low pressure,
quite a frequent occurrence in an unstable air mass.
The intensity of the trough can vary greatly: the cloud
and rain may pass in ten minutes or take several
hours. On a satellite picture a minor trough is seen as
a fairly narrow band of cumulus cloud. On a weather
chart the plotted observations will show falling pressure ahead of the trough and rising pressure behind
it, maybe no more than 2 or 3 millibars down and up
for a minor trough, with stations situated near the line
of the trough reporting a shower. In terms of wind, a
back of 5 to 10 degrees might be observed over a
distance of 5 to 30 miles ahead of the trough, and a
veer of about the same amount as it passes.

Some of the most interesting features are the long
bands of high cloud stretching from horizon to horizon
with high-level winds blowing along them, sometimes
at high speeds – maybe as much as 200 knots. Such
clouds can be very useful predictors (see photo-
graph). If the band of high cloud is stationary the
weather is unlikely to change in the next twelve hours
or so. If the band is the forward edge of increasing or
thickening high cloud it tells of an advancing trough,

usually a front, and its associated depression. Conversely, if the high cloud is moving away and the sky
clearing it suggests that the trough has passed and
better weather is on the way. These observations
can be further supported by noting, if possible, the
direction of movement of high cloud. If the wind aloft
in an advancing area of high cloud is markedly
veered on the surface wind (usually 90 degrees or
more) it is a certain sign of an approaching trough,
usually a warm front. Conversely, observations of the
high cloud associated with a cold front which has just
passed reveal upper winds which are markedly
backed on the surface wind. We saw the reasons for
this in chapter 4.

7 Tropical cyclones

There is one kind of cyclone that derives virtually all its energy from the release of latent heat when condensation occurs. This is the tropical cyclone, otherwise known as a hurricane in the Atlantic, or typhoon in the Pacific.

These storms rely on the processes of evaporation and condensation. Evaporation takes water vapour and heat from the sea, while condensation releases them into the atmosphere. The necessary rate of evaporation occurs only when the sea temperature is high – at least 28°C. Such temperatures are experienced in the Atlantic only in the summer and early autumn, a period known in the Caribbean and Gulf of Mexico as 'the hurricane season'.

Tropical cyclones also need a little Coriolis force to start them spinning. So in their developing stage they are never nearer the equator than 7°N or 7°S. They usually start life as shallow depressions moving westwards south of the sub-tropical high, until they reach a suitably warm sea. As they spin, vast quantities of heat and water are released into the air and the typical 'warm core' develops with its characteristic cloud-free eye. Surrounding the eye is a solid wall of cloud extending upwards to over 15,000 metres (figure 7.1). Cooling by radiation from the top of the cloud increases the efficiency of this vast heat engine and the winds increase steadily, sometimes to over 150 knots.

Figure 7.1

Avoiding a tropical cyclone is complicated by the fact that its track is often quite tortuous. Only recently have computer models been developed which give reasonably reliable predictions. The best way to be sure of avoiding such storms is to stay away from seas where the temperature is 28°C or more. Figure 7.2 shows the average position of this isotherm in September.

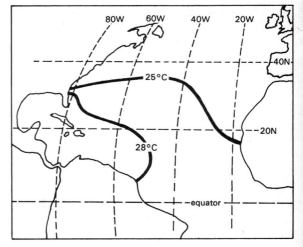

Above: Figure 7.2.
Opposite: The winds in this typhoon in the western Pacific reached over 140 knots.

8 Sources of weather information

The weather is global, and to forecast it more than two days in advance with any accuracy it is essential to take into account information from every part of the world. Every country has its own national meteorological service managing a network of observing stations, and providing weather information at least twice a day (at 0000 and 1200 GMT) for the benefit of every other country. The World Meteorological Organisation (WMO) which organises this exchange is probably the most efficient and effective of all the specialised agencies of the United Nations. The amount of information exchanged, most of it within 2½ hours from the time of observation, is vast. At Bracknell in England, one of the key communications centres for the WMO, over 200 million items of weather information are received every day. These are checked, re-broadcast, analysed, and used in millions of calculations to produce basic weather forecasts.

The weather maps you are most likely to see displayed in a foreign port are a locally produced one covering the forecast for the next few hours, and forecast charts for the outlook produced by Bracknell or the European Centre for Medium Range Weather Forecasting. Known as the ECMWF or EC for short, this is based only a few miles from Bracknell and has similar computng resources, but its forecasts are updated only once daily based on 1200 GMT observations. Bracknell's forecasts are updated globally twice daily based on 0000 and 1200 GMT, and regionally following receipt of data for 0600 and 1800 GMT. In practice this gives four new shipping bulletins daily. These bulletins are fine-tuned by referring to the latest observations made hourly at points over and around Britain.

There are a variety of ways of distributing all this weather information to the user. Let us look at each in turn.

Newspapers

Most newspapers publish a weather forecast of sorts, provided by either the National Met Service or a consultant. The most detailed and comprehensive are found in the broadsheet newspapers. The forecast itself is a good few hours old by the time you read it – written at about 2200 the previous day or earlier – but the printed weather maps are very useful. Your weather observations are ten times more useful when studied in the context of a weather map showing the positions of the main weather systems. So cut out and study the sequence of weather maps for several days before you set sail. See how the lows and highs are developing and moving. Get a feel for the general character of the weather. A particular weather 'mood' often persists for several weeks with similar sequences tending to repeat themselves. You can also compare the actual and forecast charts for the same time – some newspapers publish both, some only one. This way you will be tuned in to what the weather is doing, and much better able to prepare your own weather map from broadcast information received at sea.

Television

Watching personal presentations by weather forecasters helps to improve your mental picture of the weather sequences before you set sail. Times of broadcast tend to change so check the programming details. Always try to write down the most relevant information; impressions can be unreliable.

Telephone

Facilities to speak personally to a weather forecaster have become less readily available in most countries, except on payment or by pre-arrangement. Specialist dial-up forecasts have been introduced in a number of countries, however, and details of these will be found in RYA booklet G5. Marinecall in the UK is a particularly good service with a comprehensive menu of sailing forecasts for coastal waters prepared by the nearest Met Office Weather Centre. A planning outlook for five days ahead is included.

Radio

Whether you are ashore preparing to sail, or at sea, you cannot afford to miss the radio weather bulletins, particularly the comprehensive forecasts for shipping and sailing broadcast by many European countries on national radio networks as well as from coast radio stations. Times, frequencies, etc. are subject to

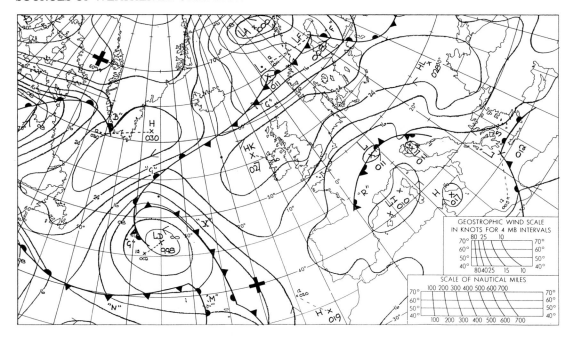

Figure 8.1: A facsimile chart.

change, but the details given in G5 are updated every year.

Facsimile

A number of countries offer a full 24-hour broadcast schedule of actual and forecast weather maps for reception by radio facsimile machines, some of them specifically intended for shipping. The most useful for European waters are listed in G5. Comprehensive details are provided in the Admiralty List of Radio Signals (ALRS) Vol. 3, and in an annual publication by Klingenfaus, in English, which some find easier to follow. For Europe the Bracknell, Northwood and Offenbach broadcasts are the most useful. Northwood, the broadcast for the Royal Navy, is based on information from Bracknell.

More than half the charts broadcast by radio facsimile are for aviation and relate to winds and temperatures high up. Those you want are labelled 'surface' or identified by the letter 'S' in a coded heading. If the letters 'S' and 'U' appear together there will be two sets of lines, one for the surface and the other relating to the upper air. Other widely used identifiers are 'VT' for 'validity times', and 'PROG' for 'prognosis'. 'T+0' means the actual weather map for the time, 'T+24' a 24-hour forecast, 'T+48' a 48 hour (2-day) forecast, 'T+72' a 3-day forecast, and so on.

Some charts, those from Bracknell in particular, include a geostrophic wind scale in one corner. The geostrophic wind is the meteorologists' name for the wind arising from the balance between the pressure gradient and Coriolis forces. To use the geostrophic scale to obtain the surface wind speed in an area, put your dividers on two adjacent isobars within the area concerned and transfer them to the scale with one point at the left-hand side. Then read the wind speed appropriate to the latitude and subtract 10 per cent to 20 per cent to obtain the surface wind: 10 per cent if the air is unstable, 20 per cent or more if the air is stable.

Some facsimile charts include plotted surface observations. These are always 'actual' charts for the time shown. If reception is good you may be able to read the details of these observations. The key to interpreting them is on page 41.

Navtex

If you have the appropriate machine on board, it will automatically receive warnings of gale, storm and other hazards. Details are given in G5.

GMDSS

The Global Marine Distress and Safety Service includes a twice-daily wind and weather forecast for all high seas in addition to warnings of gales and storms. It is broadcast on Inmarsat Standard C.

9 Using the weather bulletins

You may be tempted to skip this chapter and turn to the next one, believing that the practical skills needed to draw a weather map are beyond you. But in reality the sort of precision normally associated with science is quite unnecessary. The shipping bulletin is not a precise definition of a weather situation, merely information from which you have to tease out as many clues as possible about the winds where you are sailing. The only bit of theory you need to know is that there is a relationship between the pressure pattern and the wind, and that the surface wind over the sea blows slightly across the isobars towards low pressure.

The following paragraphs describe the process of drawing a map for the whole area covered by the shipping bulletin. However, having considered the positions and movements of the major features given in the general synopsis you may prefer to construct only the part of the weather map around the area where you are. Not too small an area, of course; at least 200 miles upwind of your position and 100 miles downwind is recommended.

Do not start drawing your weather map until you have some idea of what shape it should be. Always refer back to the most recent available chart; the one you drew yourself or the one in the newspaper. Starting from scratch is very difficult, even for a professional meteorologist.

The first step is to establish the general shape of the pressure pattern using the observations of pressure and wind. In my experience it is best to use feathery pencil lines to sketch the approximate positions of the isobars, making some lines darker than others as you approach the solution. Do not be put off by the skill and precision with which some charts are drawn. Your solution is likely to be just as useful.

USING THE SHIPPING BULLETIN

There is a great deal more to be gleaned from a shipping bulletin than simply the forecast of wind speed and direction for the particular area in which you are sailing. The information for all the other areas, together with the latest observations from a selection of coastguard stations, lighthouses, lightvessels and buoys, is sufficient to reconstruct the weather map for the whole area over and around the British Isles, thus setting the forecast for your area in context, and providing a basis for judging variations in the wind and weather which may affect your passage.

A forecaster when writing the forecast for shipping will consult two weather maps; one called an 'actual' for the latest main observing time available (0000, 0600, 1200, 1800 GMT) and the other a forecast chart for 24 hours later than this time. The 'general synopsis' describes briefly the important features of these charts, and the forecast which is given for sea areas all around the country is a synthesis of what these two charts show, starting with what the weather is now through to what is expected in 24 hours time. You can with a little practice reverse this procedure, and working backwards from the forecast reconstruct the essential parts of both the charts the forecaster started with.

The easiest and most useful application of the shipping bulletin, however, is to construct a single weather map for the time for which the observations are given, i.e. a time *between* the times of the two maps used by the forecaster. For instance, for the shipping bulletin broadcast at about 1400 the forecaster will be looking at an 'actual' chart for 0600 GMT and a forecast chart for 0600 GMT the following day. The observations given in the bulletin will be for 1200. So you can construct a chart for 1200 using the observations and interpolating for this time the position of weather systems and the strength and directions of the winds from the forecast. The following table relates the various times – clock times except the 'actual' charts which are always GMT.

	approx time of bulletin broadcast			
	0100	0600	1400	1800
Time of latest 'actual' chart described in general synopsis	1800	0000	0600	1200
Approx time forecast issued	0000	0500	1300	1700
Time of coastal station reports	2300	0400	1200	1600
Time for which you draw map	2300	0400	1200	1600

The steps to this reconstruction are as follows. Recommended techniques, abbreviations, etc. are described on pages 41–44.

1 Transcribe the shipping bulletin. The prepared 'Metmap' form published jointly by the Royal Meteorological Society and the RYA is recommended.
2 Take a blank map of the area – again, the specially prepared Metmaps are by far the easiest to use.
3 Write down the values of pressure and wind given in the bulletin alongside the positions of each of the observing points, and make sure you also write down somewhere on the chart the time at which the observations were made. Include your own observation as well.
4 Plot the positions of highs and lows and their pressure values from the general synopsis. Also sketch in the positions of troughs and ridges if any are given. Note that you are reconstructing a weather map for the time at which the observations were made at the coastal stations. This means interpolating the values and positions of the highs, lows, fronts, etc., between the start time in the general synopsis – usually 4 to 6 hours earlier – and the end time, which is usually 19 or 20 hours later than the time of the observations.
5 Write in each sea area the wind speed and direction appropriate to the time of the observations.
6 You now have a lot of wind information on your chart and a selection of pressure values. From these, sketch in the isobars to fit the pressure values, aligned so that the wind is blowing along them but slightly inwards towards low pressure and outwards from high pressure, and so that their distance apart is inversely proportional to the wind speed. It is best to use standard values for the isobars starting from 1000 mb and at intervals of 4 mb (2 mb if the wind is light).
7 Add any relevant information gleaned from other bulletins.
8 Don't forget that wind directions and strengths reported from coastal stations may be influenced by local coastal effects and sea or land breezes, so that they may not fit the isobars. You will have to work it out. Winds from lightvessels far from land are more reliable.

TERMINOLOGY

Gale warnings

Warnings are issued for:
  Gales. If the mean wind is expected to increase to force 8 (34 knots) or over, or gusts of 43 knots or over are expected. Gusts as high as 43 knots may occur with the mean wind below 34 knots in cold, unstable and showery airstreams.
  Severe gales. If the mean wind is expected to increase to force 9 (41 knots) or over, or gusts of 52 knots or over are expected.
  Storm. If the mean wind is expected to increase to force 10 (48 knots) or over, or gusts of 62 knots are expected.
  The words 'imminent', 'soon', and 'later', have precise meanings as follows:
  Imminent – within 6 hours of issue of the warning.
  Soon – 6–12 hours from time of issue.
  Later – beyond 12 hours from time of issue.

Wind

In sea area forecasts, winds are always given in terms of the Beaufort scale (see table overleaf). In land area forecasts, winds are described as moderate, fresh, etc. and these terms are defined as follows:

Description	Beaufort Force
calm	0
light	1–3
moderate	4
fresh	5
strong	6–7
gale	8

Visibility

In sea area forecasts visibility descriptions have the following meanings:

Description	Extent of visibility
good	more than 5 nautical miles
moderate	2 to 5 nautical miles
poor	1000 metres to 2 nautical miles
fog	less than 1000 metres

In land area forecasts the fog limit is lower and the following terms are used:

Description	Extent of visibility
mist	visibility 200 to 1100 yards
fog	visibility less than 200 yards
dense fog	visibility less than 50 yards

In coastal station reports and also in aviation forecasts the definitions are:

Description	Extent of visibility
mist or haze	1000 to 2000 metres
fog	less than 1000 metres

Beaufort scale of wind force

Beaufort No.	General Description	At sea	On land	Limits of velocity in knots
0	Calm	Sea like a mirror.	Calm; smoke rises vertically.	Less than 1
1	Light air	Ripples.	Direction of wind shown by smoke drift but not by wind vanes.	1 to 3
2	Light breeze	Small wavelets.	Wind felt on face; leaves rustle.	4 to 6
3	Gentle breze	Large wavelets. Crests begin to break.	Leaves and small twigs in constant motion. Wind extends light flags.	7 to 10
4	Moderate	Small waves becoming longer, fairly frequent white horses.	Raises dust and loose paper; small branches are moved.	11 to 16
5	Fresh breeze	Moderate waves, many white horses, chance of some spray.	Small trees in leaf begin to sway.	17 to 21
6	Strong breeze	Large waves begin to form; the white foam crests are more extensive everywhere. Probably some spray.	Large branches in motion Umbrellas used with difficulty.	22 to 27
7	Near gale	Sea heaps up and white foam from breaking waves begins to be blown in streaks along the direction of the wind.	Whole trees in motion	28 to 33
8	Gale	Moderately high waves of greater length; edges of crests begin to break into spin-drift. The foam is blown in well-marked streaks along the direction of the wind.	Breaks twigs off trees; generally impedes progress	34 to 40
9	Severe gale	High waves. Crests of waves begin to topple, tumble and roll over. Spray may affect visibility.	Slight structural damage (chimney-pots and slates removed).	41 to 47
10	Storm	Very high waves with long overhanging crests.	Seldom experienced inland trees uprooted, considerable structural damage occurs.	48 to 55
11	Violent storm			56 to 63
12	Hurricane			Greater than 63

Weather

This is not included in reports from automatic stations. In reports where it does appear the terms 'rain', 'snow', 'hail', etc., are obvious enough but the use of the word 'fair' needs defining. The weather is described as 'fair' when there is nothing 'significant' happening, i.e. no rain, fog, showers, etc. It may or may not be cloudy.

Pressure and pressure tendency

The general synopsis often gives the values of the pressure at the centres of the important weather systems, while the coastal station reports give recorded atmospheric pressure and also the pressure tendency. The international unit for measuring pressure is the millibar, sometimes known as the hecto-pascal. The terms used for pressure tendency in the coastal station reports are defined as follows:

Description	Pressure tendency
steady	change less than 0.1mb in 3 hours
rising slowly (falling slowly)	change 0.1 to 1.5mb in last 3 hours
rising (falling)	change 1.6 to 3.5mb in last 3 hours
rising quickly (falling quickly)	change 3.6 to 6.0mb in last 3 hours
rising (falling) very rapidly	change of more than 6.0mb in last 3 hours
now falling (now rising)	change from rising to falling (and vice versa) within last 3 hours

One must beware of reading too much into reports of 'rising slowly' and 'falling slowly', and also 'now falling' and 'now rising', if general pressure changes are small. Every day there are small ups and downs in pressure all over the world due to the atmospheric tide. In the south of Britain the tidal pressure variation is just under 1 mb. At the equator it is 3 mb. The highest values of pressure due to this tide occur at 1000 and 2200, the lowest at 0400 and 1600: the same local times everywhere in the world. So if at 0400 or 1600 the pressure is reported as 'falling slowly' it does not mean the weather is likely to or beginning to deteriorate. Similarly if at 1000 or 2200 the pressure is reported as 'rising slowly' it says nothing about improvement in the weather.

State of sea

Definition	Height of waves (metres)
Calm – glassy	0
calm – rippled	0 to 0.1
smooth	0.1 to 0.5
slight	0.5 to 1.25
moderate	1.25 to 2.5
rough	2.5 to 4
very rough	4 to 6
high	6 to 9
very high	9 to 14
phenomenal	Over 14

TRANSCRIBING SHIPPING BULLETINS

Even if you transcribe a shipping bulletin in long-hand you will still need to use some form of abbreviation to put the information on your weather map. There is much to be said for using the same short-hand throughout. There is nothing to stop you devising your own shorthand so long as you can remember afterwards the meaning of what you have written, but I recommend using a notation which has been evolved by those with considerable experience in using shipping bulletins and which includes a number of the standard international weather map symbols. Once you are familiar with the more common of these international symbols you will be able to appreciate at a glance the information contained on any weather map which you may see displayed in clubs or at ports of call.

Abridged Beaufort weather notation and international plotting symbols		
Weather	Beaufort letter	plotting symbol
rain	r	●
drizzle	d	，
snow	s	✳
shower	p	▽
hail	h	△
thunderstorm	ph	⏃
squall	q	⋎
mist	m	=
fog	f	≡
haze	z	∞

The general synopsis

Few international symbols are involved here except for the points of the compass – N, S, NW, SW etc. Initial letters are the best shorthand for weather systems – L for low, H for high and so on. One very useful hint is to use a vertical stroke or solidus to denote the passage of time. Movement is best denoted by an arrow. Thus 'a depression 996 mb over Faeroes at 1200 today is expected over German Bight 978 mb by 1200 tomorrow' is written as 'L 996 Faer/ 978 G Bt'.

Sea area forecasts

Winds are always transcribed in terms of points of the compass and force, and using the solidus for the passage of time, a sentence such as 'northwest 4 to 5 at first backing south-west and increasing to 7 to gale 8 by the end of the period' is written simply as 'NW 4–5/SW 7–8'. Similarly 'in the south at first' is written 'in S/' and 'in the north later' as '/in N'.

Weather

This is always given in terms such as 'fair', 'showers', 'rain', etc. Here international shorthand should be used and you can choose between the Beaufort letter notation or the international weather map symbols as given above. There is something to be said for using the international map symbols because you can then plot these directly on to your map, but the former are much easier to learn and you can readily turn them into plotting symbols at your leisure after the broadcast. The phrases 'at first', and 'later', are often used and, again, a vertical stroke or solidus comes in very useful. For instance 'rain at first, showers later', can be abbreviated to 'r/p'. This sort of detail should always be taken down as it almost certainly ties in with a change of wind and the passage of an important weather system through the sea area.

For heavy precipitation, capital letters are used, e.g. R – heavy rain.

Visibility

A straightforward abbreviation of 'g' for 'good', 'm' for 'moderate' and 'p' for 'poor' is all that is required here, remembering again to use a vertical stroke to denote passage of time and also to take down all the details which are given about fog.

Coastal station reports

As with the sea area forecasts you need a prepared form with the coastal stations already listed, and columns for the reports which are always given for each station in the following sequence:
● wind
● significant weather – not included in reports from automatic stations. (Fair and fine are not 'significant' and are not mentioned.)
● visibility in miles or metres
● barometric pressure in millibars
● pressure tendency (i.e. whether the barometer is rising or falling and how rapidly).

The same shorthand should be used as for the sea area forecasts. There is no need to write down the words 'miles' or 'metres' as one- or two-digit figures will always be metres. Writing down the value of

pressure it saves time to use only the last two digits – anything over 50 will normally be 9—, and anything under 50 will be 10—. The pressure tendency should be abbreviated with the initial letters or you can use a stroke inclined at various angles according to the way you would observe the movement of pressure on a barograph.

DRAWING A WEATHER MAP

Having taken down the information, your next step is to plot it on a weather chart. Throughout the world there is a standard format for doing this. The wind is always drawn as a feathered arrow blowing towards the observing position and with the 'feathers' always on the clockwise side of the arrow. The number of feathers is always proportional to the wind strength. For winds given in Beaufort force use one feather for force 2, one and a half for force 3 and so on. The rest of the information is accommodated around the observing position like this:

So northwest 5, continuous slight rain, 2 miles, 1009 millibars, falling is plotted like this:

Similarly plot the wind and the weather in each one of the sea areas, using more than one plot as necessary depending on the amount of information given. For instance a forecast for sea areas Forties of 'northwest 4 to 5 in east, 6 to 7 in west, showers, good' is plotted:

It is best to plot the average or highest value, but remember that you have done so when fitting the isobars.

Drawing the isobars

We know that the pressure gradient, which on a weather map is given by the distance apart of the

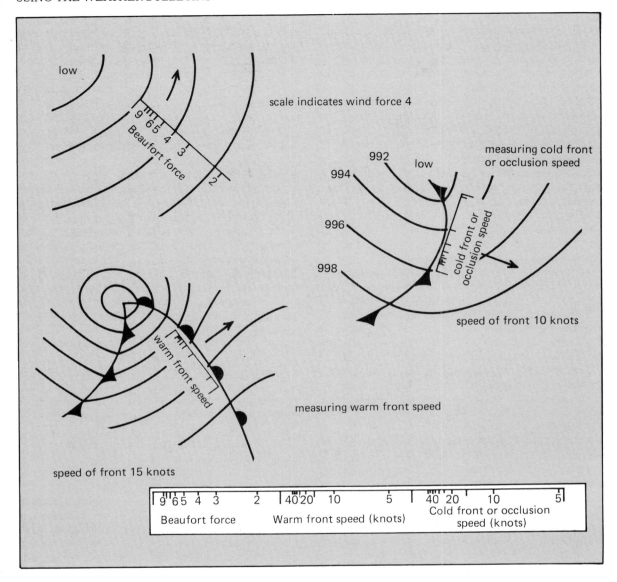

Figure 9.1 – Using the speed scale published with the Metmap.

isobars, is inversely proportional to the wind speed. So we can devise a simple scale relating wind speed to the distance apart of the isobars and use it either to derive the wind speed from isobars already drawn, or, given the wind speed, to draw the isobars the right distance apart. The scale we use must be related to the distance scale appropriate to the map projection. Most charts used for drawing weather maps have a scale printed in one corner. The example in figure 9.1 is taken from the Metmap.

The relationship between pressure gradient and surface wind speed is slightly dependent on latitude and the curvature of the isobars, and also on whether the air is stable or unstable. The scale on the Metmap assumes straight isobars over a sea surface and marginally unstable conditions. It is reasonably valid between 40 degrees N and 60 degrees N. Allow for lighter winds than prescribed in higher latitudes, in strongly curved isobars around a low and also in stable conditions. Allow for stronger winds than prescribed in lower latitudes, in strongly curved isobars around a high and in unstable conditions.

So, referring if possible to a previous weather map, either in the newspaper or one you drew yourself, draw the new positions of the isobars starting where you have observed pressure values and then extending outwards to the known positions of centres of low and high pressure, all the time using your dividers to get the isobars approximately the right distance apart according to the scale. Over sea areas the isobars should be aligned to the wind so that it is blowing almost parallel to them but slightly towards low pressure. Keep to standard values for the isobars, usually every 4 mb up or down from 1000 mb, or in light winds every 2 mb, and remember that reported pressure values are rounded up or down to the nearest mb, so you have a bit of latitude in where to put the lines.

Drawing the fronts and troughs

Here considerations of continuity are particularly useful. Where was the front 24 or 12 hours ago? What position, if any, was given in the shipping bulletin? What is the wind component at right angles to it? How far is it likely to have moved from its last known position up to the time for which you are constructing the chart? Is this compatible with the forecast position?

The scale you use for relating the wind speed to the distance apart of the isobars can be adapted to measure the speed of a front or trough. The instantaneous speed of these features is proportional to the wind component at right angles to their line of advance. Cold fronts and typical troughs in cold air move relatively faster than warm fronts. A scale is provided in the corner of the Metmap and figure 9.1 shows how to use it.

The latest observations are also important. Do the differences in wind direction, weather, and pressure tendency between one side of the front (trough) and the other support your analysis? The table will remind you of the typical changes at a front or trough.

	Trough	Warm front	Cold front
wind	veers	veers	veers
visibility	–	decreases	increases
weather	clearance	drizzle or fair	clearance
	after rain	after rain	after rain
pressure	rise after fall	steady after fall	rise after fall

Finally, having determined the position of the trough or front, identify it with the standard symbols: a dotted line for a trough, and for a front a solid line with blobs or spikes protruding from its leading edge depending on whether it is a warm or cold front.

You will then need to redraw the isobars at the fronts so that they show a clear discontinuity. Indeed you will often wish to sketch in the positions of fronts and troughs before you start drawing the isobars.

USING YOUR WEATHER MAP

Having drawn your weather map you will have a very much better understanding of the weather situation and a much better ability to interpret the naked forecast than if you had just written down the forecasts for your sea area. For instance, the forecast wind may be southwesterly force 5. It may be critical for a long beat to windward to know whether 'southwesterly' means 220 degrees or 240 degrees. Your map will help you decide. It will also indicate whether force 6 is more likely over one side of the sea area than the other, or later rather than sooner. When the direction is given as 'south-west to west' your map may reveal a bend in the isobars with west at one side of the area and southwest at the other; or alternatively it may reveal a weak trough which you can expect to be moving through the area. A multitude of minor inferences are possible which taken over a season make your sailing safer, more skilful and more enjoyable.

At the end of this book are two examples of forecasts and their associated weather maps.

USING THE OBSERVATIONS

It is always useful to make a special study of the observations available from places close to where you are sailing.

If you are in a rapidly changing weather situation, typically a westerly one with a series of depressions, troughs and ridges moving through your area, it is the observations upwind which are most important and you need to look carefully at those up to two hundred miles away, if not more.

If the weather is slow-moving, particularly if it is anticyclonic and the wind is force 4 or less, careful attention to all observations within a hundred miles or so will pay dividends. Plot them all on your weather map and follow them through in time sequence noting the changes in pressure, wind direction, wind speed and visibility. Make allowance for the 'tidal effect' in pressure values, and for night and day coastal effects on the wind, e.g. land and sea breezes. You are very likely to identify small changes or bends in pressure gradient and in wind which are too small to be men-

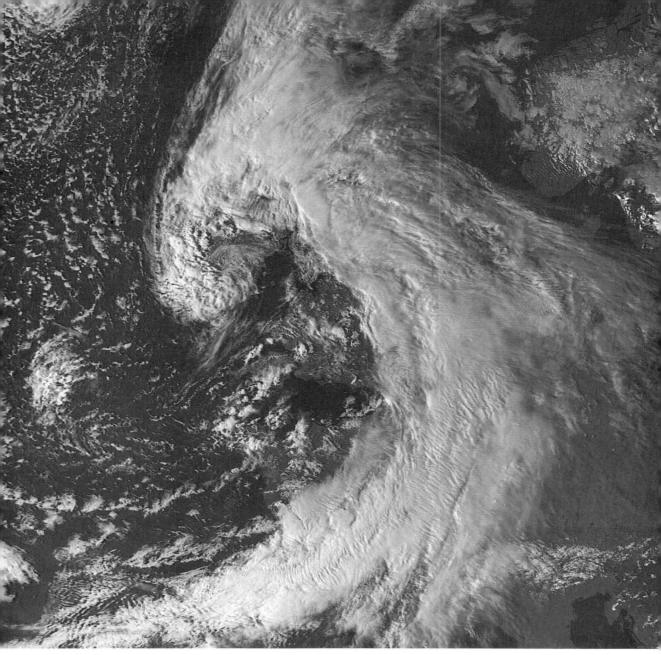

tioned in the shipping bulletin. For instance, observations from lightvessels may reveal eddies in the
wind of the order of 5 to 15 miles across. Such eddies
are found only in relatively light winds, and more
often than not they are the dying remnants of an
afternoon sea-breeze circulation which continues to
drift out seawards long after the sun has gone down.
They may be found as far as fifty miles or more off
the coast. Never say, "I don't believe it, it doesn't fit".
It is not unknown for an observation to be wrong –
but it is very rare.

*Above: The clouds of a deep depression centred over
northern Ireland. A cold front lies from the north Irish
Sea across northern and eastern England and central
France to northeast Spain. Time 1513 on 1 September
1988, 24 hours after the picture on page 12. The weather
map for three hours earlier is on page 14. As the low
has deepened the cloud ahead of the cold front has
become organised into a more solid band.*

10 Making your own observations

Your own weather observation is just as important as any other weather observation. It is unique to you and demands a place on your weather map. It is part of the overall weather picture, and whereas over land there is a good network of weather stations, at sea there are hardly any. Forecasters attempt to fill in the gaps by studying pictures from weather satellites, but although these are a great help they do not provide the 'ground truth' for where you are. You can supply this by making your own observations.

Enter your observations in your log at regular intervals, preferably at times which coincide with a weather chart, either a fax chart which will be for one of the 'main hours GMT', i.e. 0000, 0600, 1200, or 1800; or the charts you construct yourself which will be for an 'intermediate' hour appropriate to the time of the coastal station reports included in the bulletin. If the weather is changing rapidly it will be worth making more frequent log entries.

You should observe and log the following:

1 Wind direction. An observation using hand-bearing compass and tell-tale will need correcting for boat movement.

2 Wind speed. An on-deck observation using a hand-held anenometer will need correcting for boat movement. If you have no instrument judge the wind speed in terms of Beaufort Force by looking at the sea surface and referring to the definitions on page 40.

Remember that there will be a difference between masthead and deck readings of both wind speed and direction, depending on the height of your mast and the stability of the air. The deck reading will be the lighter and more backed.

3 Atmospheric pressure. It is the changes in pressure that matter most, but it does help to have your barometer or barograph reading correctly so that your observation fits the others on your weather map. Therefore it is worth checking your pressure reading with the nearest weather centre before you leave harbour and making any adjustments necessary.

4 If you have a barograph, record whether the pressure is rising, falling or steady.

5 Visibility – in general terms (good, very good, poor).

6 Clouds. Keep your eye on the sky. Get used to looking at the clouds, the high ones as well as the low ones, and judging their speed of movement – not in absolute terms, but merely whether they are moving fast or slowly and from which direction. The clouds hold many clues to the weather in the next few hours.

7 State of sea. Note particularly the height, period (time between wave crests) and direction of any swell.

If you have a thermometer or hygrometer log their readings as well. The temperature of the sea water can be of interest too, especially if there is a risk of fog (chapter 15) or you need more wind (chapter 14). Part of a ship's weather log is shown opposite.

USING YOUR WEATHER OBSERVATION

Having made your observation, study it in relation to the latest available weather map – either the official version or one you constructed yourself. If the times are reasonably coincident plot the observation on the map and see how it fits. If the wind speed and direction are within 20 per cent and 20 degrees of the figures indicated by the isobars you can be reasonably confident that you have the overall picture of the weather. But if they do not fit, do not tear up the weather map or the forecast. Your observation cannot invalidate all the other information which went into the weather analysis and forecasting process.

Let us look at some possible reasons for a large discrepancy in wind speed and/or direction (a large discrepancy in pressure is much less likely).

1 If the wind is light – force 1 or 2 – it is not unusual to find an eddy, perhaps two or three miles across, moving downwind at about the same speed as the general wind given by the pressure pattern. It might take up to an hour to cross you, and if your course and speed are the same as that of the eddy it could take much longer.

2 Is it a coastal effect? A sea or land breeze, for instance? These are not normally included in shipping bulletins, and they do not conform to the isobaric map.

0900   Wind WSW force 3, pressure 1008 mb, half cover cloud, slight
       swell from SW, visibility good.
1015   Light shower
1200   Wind SW force 4, pressure 1007 mb, cloud increasing from
       west, swell from SW increasing, visibility good.
1345   Rain started, wind backed to SSW and increased to
       force 5, barometer falling more rapidly, now 1005 mb.
1500   Wind SSW force 5, raining quite heavily, pressure
       1004 mb, steady swell from SW, visibility poor
1520   Rain stopped, wind veered to WSW force 4, pressure
       now rising, clear sky to west, steady swell from
       SW, good visibility.

3 Is it a detached remnant of a sea breeze? This is an interesting and far from unusual phenomenon. Following a good sea breeze day the seaward end of the sea breeze may break away as night falls and continue to move out seawards on the offshore gradient wind. Such an eddy may be from 2 to 10 miles across and will give a completely different wind for an hour or two.

4 Is it due to a thunderstorm or heavy shower? During its lifetime of 2–3 hours such a storm is likely to generate its own winds. One wind will be taking air into the storm and another, usually preceded by a squall, will be taking cold air out of it.

If your observation disagrees with the forecast but fits the weather map, then it is worth checking that the forecast was for the area you are in. Did you write down the forecast or are you working from memory?

11 Winds near coasts

Wind blowing off the shore

If the wind is blowing from the land, whatever the angle of the wind to the land, the direction of the wind will always veer and the speed increase as it moves out over the water (figure 11.1). Some books state incorrectly that the effect is one of refraction, and that the wind changes direction towards a line at right angles to the land. This is not so. We have already seen that for a given pressure gradient wind the difference between the direction of the surface wind over land and over water is about 25 to 30 degrees. So whatever the angle of the wind to the shore, its direction will veer as the wind moves out over the water. This means that it often pays to make for harbour on port tack. You can expect to be headed if you approach land close-hauled on starboard.

Figure 11.1 – Wind veering over the water.

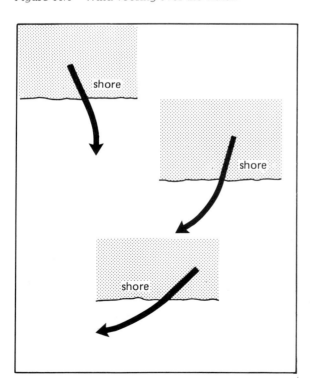

Wind blowing along the shore

You may not have noticed it, but there is a quite remarkable difference when the wind is blowing along the coast, depending on whether the land is on your left or your right-hand side when you are standing with your back to the wind.

If the coast is on your right-hand side when standing with your back to the wind, the different angles of the surface winds over land and water are convergent for the same pressure gradient wind (figure 11.2). This results in a band of stronger wind within two to three miles of the shore. The increase in speed in the band is normally of the order of 25 per cent, e.g. 5 knots added on to a 20-knot wind. Also because of the convergence of the airstreams the air is forced upwards, often giving an increase in cloud or a band of thicker cloud along the coast.

The stronger wind just offshore is often mistaken for a sea breeze but in fact it persists day and night. So if you put out from harbour on the south coast of England in an easterly wind and find it force 5 instead of the expected force 4 you can be reasonably sure that by the time you are three or four miles off the coast it will have dropped to the lower speed you were hoping for. Equally, when you are approaching

Figure 11.2 Convergence.

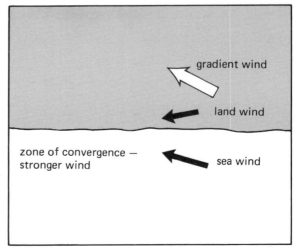

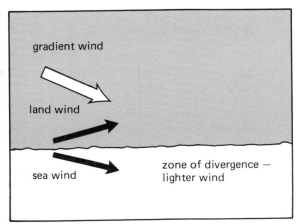

Figure 11.3 – Divergence.

a coast where the land and sea winds are converging be prepared for an increase.

When, standing with your back to the wind, the coast is on your left-hand side, the effect is the opposite (figure 11.3). The airstreams diverge, the wind is that much lighter near the shore and there is less cloud than elsewhere. This is why the sunniest seaside resorts are often found where the prevailing wind is westerly on a south-facing coast, easterly on a north-facing coast, and so on. Note however that in the afternoons this lack of wind near the coast is often overridden by a sea breeze.

Wind blowing onto the shore
There is no insignificant variation in the wind over the water. All of the changes occur over land.

Coastal cliffs
If the wind is blowing *along* the shore it makes little difference whether there are cliffs or not; the effects described above are well marked and sometimes enhanced. That is, we observe within a few miles of the coast a zone of stronger or lighter winds depending upon the wind direction.

If the wind is blowing *off* the shore, it will be affected by the cliffs (figure 11.4). Standing waves often form in the wind downwind of the cliff face and give relatively static zones of stronger and lighter wind, sometimes marked by a cloud sitting on top of the lighter wind zones. The zones of stronger wind are the more reliable and are likely to remain in nearly the same place for as long as the wind direction and stability of the airstream do not change. The zones of lighter wind may be characterised by considerable variations, even reversals in wind direction, particularly downwind of the higher cliffs, but the positions of the zones themselves are likely to stay put for some time. Beneath the cliff itself there is usually a large eddy in the flow of air with a reversal in wind direction.

An island
A mountainous island clearly obstructs the wind, and not surprisingly its influence extends many miles downwind. The Canaries are a good example. Downwind of these islands large eddies form in the air flow, often between fifty and a hundred miles across. Having formed, they move away downwind, dispersing only slowly. Satellite pictures quite often reveal a string of three or four eddies, the furthest being some two or three hundred miles away from the islands.

Figure 11.4 – Coastal cliffs.

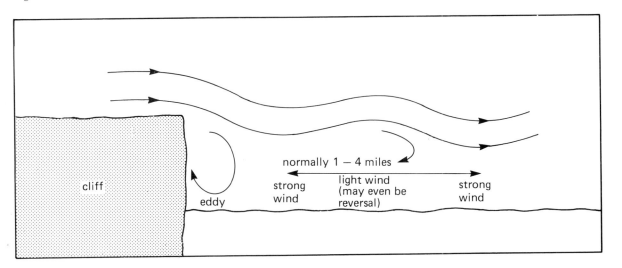

Even a small, flat island has a significant influence on the wind up to five miles or more downwind. The air flowing over it is subject to greater friction, so it slows down and its direction backs some 15 degrees. Along one side of the island a zone of stronger wind will be caused by converging airstreams, and along the other side there will be a zone of lighter wind caused by diverging airstreams (figure 11.5).

These zones of stronger and lighter wind will not be limited to the island shore but will continue downwind for a considerable distance, perhaps tens of miles. Sometimes a line of cloud or individual clouds will provide evidence of the position of the stronger wind band, and a line of blue sky or thinner cloud evidence of the lighter wind band.

Land breezes
These are found near coasts at night or in the early morning, usually when the sky is clear. They are *not* the opposite of sea breezes. The best way to visualise them is as 'drainage' winds. Air that has cooled over the land on a clear night, being relatively dense, drains downwards, usually following valleys, until it reaches the sea. Its momentum carries it a mile or two out to sea before it warms up and dies away.

The direction of a land breeze is controlled almost entirely by the contours of the land. The cold air flows down the valleys and on reaching the sea spreads out fanwise. The steeper the slope, the stronger the breeze.

An offshore pressure gradient wind may be enhanced by a 'drainage' land breeze as described above. In the absence of a drainage wind, however, an offshore wind at night may be modified by another effect. Because the land cools at night much more than the sea, any wind due to the pressure gradient is likely to decrease at night near the land surface and may even die away altogether, while continuing almost unchanged over the open water well away from the land. Thus near the coast at night there will be a zone where the wind is picking up gradually to its open sea speed and direction.

Mountain and valley winds
In mountainous areas the pressure gradient wind can either be bent to blow along the valleys, if it is blowing somewhere near that direction, or else it will blow across the tops of the mountains, leaving only eddies in the valleys.

In addition there is frequently some form of drainage wind to be found – either as a result of cold air accumulating in the valleys, or because cold air from behind a cold front piles up against a mountain

Figure 11.5

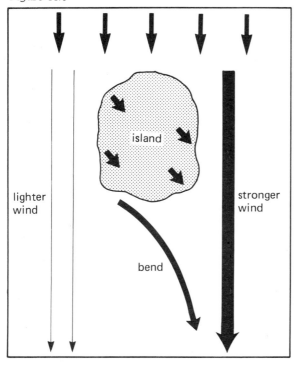

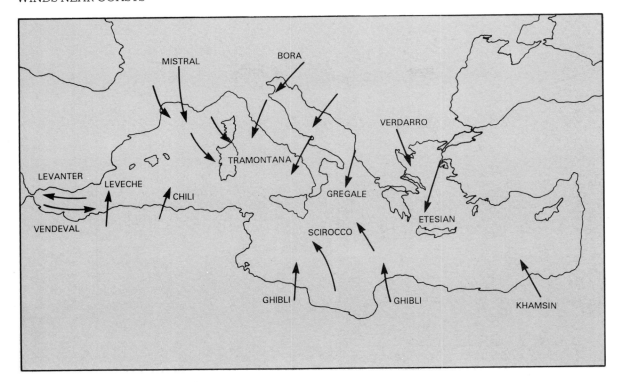

Figure 11.6 – Mediterranean winds.

barrier until it finds a way out. Both types of drainage wind can arise very suddenly, and both exhibit some diurnal variation. They are strongest in the early morning when the air is coldest, and lightest in the afternoon when the air is warmest.

MEDITERRANEAN WINDS

The most notable winds that affect the Mediterranean are essentially mountain and valley winds. The mountain ranges, from the Pyrenees in the west, through the Alps to the Taurus Mountains in the east, are high enough to block the southward movement of cold fronts. The cold air piles up against the mountains, and a day or two after the arrival of the front it starts escaping down the main valleys or through mountain gaps. The Rhone valley is one route south, and the local wind is called the *Mistral*. Normally there is enough cold air available to keep the *Mistral* going for several days, and it often contributes to the formation of a depression in the Ligurian Sea. Typically the wind strength is Force 6 to 8, sometimes severe gale Force 9.

Further east we have the *Bora* and *Tramontana* carrying cold air into the Adriatic Sea, and the *Gregale* and *Verdarro* which carry cold air into the Ionian and Aegean Seas. The *Etesian* or *Meltemi* is more feared in the Aegean: it has some of the characteristics of cold air spilling south but is essentially the funnelling of a gradient northeasterly wind from the Black Sea. It may persist for several days at a time, blowing at Force 6 to 7.

Two gap winds of the western Mediterranean are the *Vendaval* and *Levanter*. The *Vendaval* is a strong westerly emerging from the Straits of Gibraltar, and the *Levanter* a strong easterly being squeezed between Spain and Morocco as it approaches the same Straits.

The *Ghibli*, *Scirocco* and *Khamsin* are all southerlies which blow off the North African deserts; they are typically hot and dry. The *Leveche* and *Chili* are also hot winds from North Africa, but their warmth is as much due to their descent down the north slopes of the Atlas mountains as to their desert origin. Such winds are normally known as *föhn* winds.

It is interesting to note that the south coast of Turkey is unaffected by such winds. The summer months are characterised by moderate sea and land breezes, making the area ideal for sailing.

12 The sea breeze

The sea breeze is the result of air being warmed over the land more than over the sea, and this can happen not only on a sunny day but also when there is thin or patchy cloud. The first question to ask is "will the air temperature over the land be higher than over the sea?" If so, the sea breeze mechanism will begin to get under way as follows (figure 12.1).

1 The air over the land is warmed and expands.

2 This causes an excess of air (an imbalance of pressure) at some higher level, usually 300 to 1000 metres.

3 Air flows out seawards to remove the imbalance.

4 Air moves downwards (subsides) over the sea to take the place of air which is beginning to move across the shore – which is the sea breeze (5).

This simple case assumes no other wind, i.e. there is no pressure gradient.

As time goes on the sea breeze circulation extends steadily both inland and seaward. Because the breeze experiences greater drag as it moves over the land it tries to realign itself to a direction more parallel to the coast. The effect of the earth's rotation is to turn the breeze to the right in the northern hemisphere and to the left in the southern hemisphere.

The vertical extent of the breeze depends on the stability of the air. In stable air the return flow may be confined below 600 metres or so, in which case there is only limited scope for the sea breeze to develop and it is likely to be weak.

For the sailor it is the downward movement (subsidence) of the air over the sea feeding the sea breeze which is the most important feature. Indeed, one of the first clues to the beginning of a sea breeze is often the fairly sudden dissolving of low cloud just offshore, a sign of air gently subsiding in preparation for feeding the first drift of air onto the shore.

On a straight coastline, therefore, and in the absence of any pressure gradient, the steps in the development of a sea breeze are as follows:

1 Calm morning, clear sky or thin cloud. Temperature over land rises above sea surface temperature.

Figure 12.1 – The sea breeze.

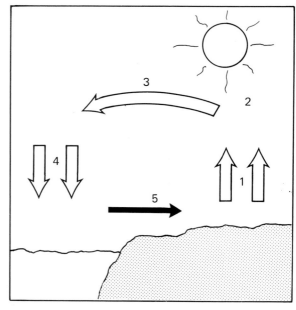

2 Cloud begins to disperse just offshore.

3 Gentle drift of air onto coast starts from about a quarter to half a mile offshore.

4 Breeze gradually increases and extends seawards.

5 Direction of breeze turns gradually to the right (northern hemisphere) whichever way the coast is facing, and its strength increases to about force 2 to 3 about two or three hours after the start. The strength depends on the stability of the air and the temperature difference between land and sea.

6 By mid-afternoon the direction is nearly along the shore, a shift of 50 to 60 degrees from the start, and the breeze extends up to 10 or 15 miles seawards.

7 The sea breeze dies away towards sunset, depending on the rate of fall of temperature over land. The dying remains of the sea-breeze circulation may continue to drift out seawards and may be found up to 30 or 40 miles from the shore in the middle of the night.

Figure 12.2

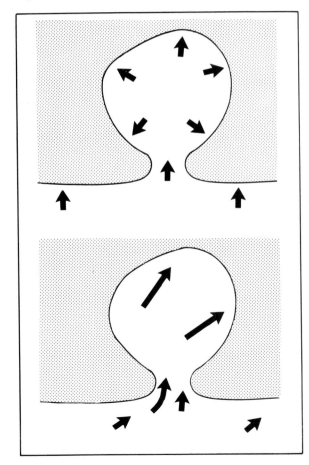

Complicated coastlines

A large bay with a narrow opening. At first the sea breeze is a drift of air onto all the shores of the bay (figure 12.2), but these onshore breezes have difficulty finding enough air to feed them and their strength pulsates between calm and 2 or 3 knots. However, some air is pulled through the entrance to the bay, and as the breezes keep trying to blow onto the shores so the amount of air pulled through the entrance increases. At the same time the sea breeze develops onto shores adjacent to the bay and eventually, so long as the bay is reasonably small, takes over the whole area. For most of the time it will be found that the right-hand shore of the bay has more wind, also that the breeze through the entrance is likely to be somewhat stronger than elsewhere, with a tendency for convergence of air into the entrance and a bend in the wind particularly on the right-hand side.

An island. In contrast to the bay, here there is plenty of air to feed the sea breeze, but (if the island is small) hardly anywhere for it to go (figure 12.3). If the island was perfectly flat and uniform there would be a gentle onshore breeze all round and perhaps a cloud sitting over the middle. The breeze would pulsate a little, veer somewhat during the day and its strength would depend on the size of the island. In practice the sea breezes are critically dependent on the topography, and even small hills, bays and valleys will cause good local breezes at the expense of calms elsewhere.

An island near the mainland. In this case the mainland sea breeze will gradually take over and eventually swamp the more local breezes onto the island, though not before there have been successive stages

Figure 12.3

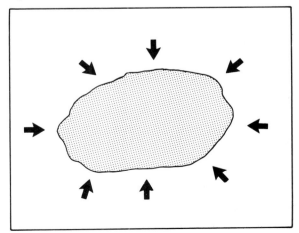

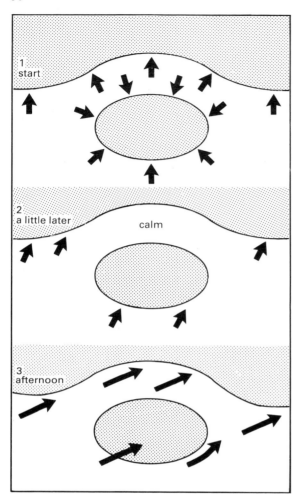

Figure 12.4

Figure 12.5

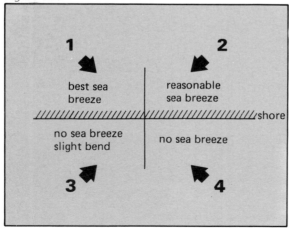

of light wind and calm over the more enclosed area of water as breezes try to blow onto all shores. A pattern is shown in figure 12.4.

So we see that as a general rule when there is no gradient wind, and however complicated the coastline, the sea breeze will start as gentle breezes blowing onshore and then develop into a breeze whose direction largely irons out the minor features of the shoreline, veering slowly until the direction is some 20 degrees from the overall line of the coast.

SEA BREEZE WITH GRADIENT WIND BLOWING

Let us see how the sea breeze is affected by a gradient wind already blowing. We know that two essential components of the sea breeze circulation are:
- An opposite (offshore) breeze blowing at some height above the surface.
- The subsidence of air over the coastal water.

In the absence of a pressure gradient there is no hindrance or help to either of these components and we experience a sea breeze whenever the temperature of the land rises to a value above the sea surface temperature. One degree difference is sufficient. But when there is a pressure gradient wind – and there usually is in Britain – the onset of a sea breeze is critically dependent on whether this initial wind is blowing offshore and encouraging the upper part of the sea breeze circulation. This only applies if the pressure gradient wind is less than about 25 knots; if it is stronger than this, a sea breeze will never develop.

Onshore gradient wind
With a gradient wind blowing onshore you never get a true sea breeze because it prevents the return flow aloft. However, the afternoon wind will be influenced by the heating of the land and will either increase or decrease as shown in figure 12.6.

Offshore gradient wind
The development of a sea breeze with an offshore gradient wind involves a calm period as the offshore wind dies away and makes way for the sea breeze blowing onshore. The behaviour of this calm patch depends on which way the offshore wind is angled to the shoreline. A divergent zone (see page 49) encourages the subsidence that feeds the onshore sea breeze. This builds up quickly and the calm zone (which appears close inshore) moves out seawards

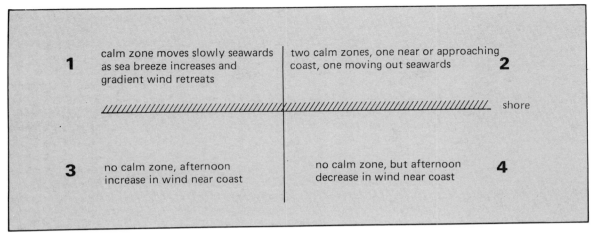

Figure 12.6

(figure 12.7). A zone of convergence opposes this subsidence and leads to a more complicated sea breeze, starting further out to sea and separated from the gradient wind by two calm zones, one moving shorewards and the other seawards (figure 12.8).

The likelihood of a sea breeze and the behaviour of the associated calm zones are summarised in figures 12.5 and 12.6, in which the possible directions of the gradient wind are split into four quadrants by a line drawn perpendicular to the coast. It is immaterial which direction the coast itself is facing; the diagrams apply equally to coasts facing north, south, east or west and all directions in between.

Some analysts trying to fit their observations of sea breezes into a pattern have sought to distinguish different sorts of sea breeze. They talk of local sea breezes and ocean sea breezes and suggest they behave differently in different places. But in fact the one critical factor on which everything else depends is the pressure gradient wind. In my experience there is just one sea breeze which generates in the same way the world over. With 360 possible directions of the gradient wind and an even greater variety of shapes of coastline, there is scope for a great variation in sea-breeze behaviour, but it is always capable of being understood as outlined here.

Figure 12.7

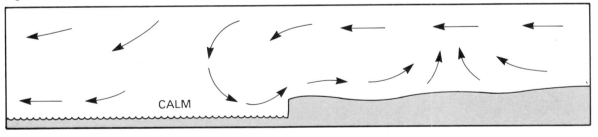

Figure 12.8

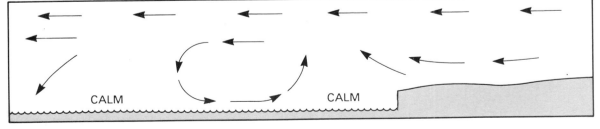

Avoiding the calms

For a gradient wind in *quadrant one* the calm period will be short and the best (strongest) afternoon wind will be found within 10 miles of the coast; but otherwise stand further off.

For a gradient wind in *quadrant two* the best night wind will be in a band within 10 miles of the coast. If this wind direction suits you then stand further off during the afternoon and avoid the calm patches. If you want a temporary blow from the opposite direction look for the sea breeze in the zone 2 to 6 miles from the land.

If the gradient wind is in *quadrant three* you will get the best afternoon wind within 6 miles of the shore; at other times stand further off.

The opposite obtains in *quadrant four*. Stand in except in the afternoon.

Complicated coastlines

The shoreline is rarely if ever straight, but do not worry too much about the complications unless you are sailing close inshore when the sea breeze is just starting. If you are, you will find that your local initial sea breeze within half a mile of the shore will relate to the orientation of the nearest shore. Thereafter the sea breeze will develop as if to smooth out the variations in the coast, and this means that you can work on the basis of the best straight line you can draw along the coast.

AFTER THE SEA BREEZE

As night falls the temperature of the land falls and the sea breeze dies – to be replaced by the offshore wind, or a calm if there is no gradient wind. The reversion to the offshore wind (*quadrants one* and *two*) usually starts inshore and moves seawards over several hours, preceded by a calm period: the stronger the offshore wind the shorter the calm. It usually pays to stay inshore, to pick up the new wind as soon as possible. This also applies in the absence of a gradient when your only chance of wind is to find the land breeze. Incidentally, do not assume that the gradient will be the same as it was when the sea breeze started. Always check with the forecast or your weather map for any larger-scale changes.

NIGHT WINDS – ONSHORE GRADIENT

In the case of an onshore gradient wind your tactics as the sun goes down will depend on whether the wind is in *quadrant three* or *quadrant four*. A *quadrant three* wind will tend to die near the shore, particularly if it is nearly parallel to the coast with the streamlines diverging, and you should stand well off. A *quadrant four* wind will increase, particularly near the shore (streamlines converging), so you should stand inshore for the best wind.

13 Winds over the open ocean

It is a misconception to think of the wind as being uniform for a given pressure gradient. It is not, even over a perfectly smooth sea – if such were possible. The wind likes blowing in bands. The most striking example of this is in the trade winds which are characterised by lines of 'trade-wind cumulus' extending over hundreds of miles. These lines of cloud are evidence of what are called 'vortex rolls' where superimposed on the horizontal motion of the air is a vertical circulation of air moving slowly up into the lines of cloud and down into the clear lanes between (figure 13.1). These cloud lanes are typically 1 to 3 miles apart and the wind somewhat stronger and more veered in the clear lanes than under the clouds.

Even in the absence of cloud, or beneath a uniformly grey and cloudy sky, wind bands will be found over the open sea. The difference in strength between adjacent light and strong bands may be anything from 10 to 25 per cent, and their distance apart from 1 to 5 miles. Near the coast the position of the bands will normally be fixed by some feature of the coast or by the coastline itself, particularly when the wind is nearly parallel to it. Well away from the coast, the bands will move slowly due to the compo-

nent of the pressure gradient wind across them (figure 13.2). Thus if you are sailing on the open sea, at least 5 miles from land, and the wind is lighter than it should be, it is advisable to sail on port tack (or gybe) until you find the stronger wind. Having found it, change to starboard tack to enable you to stay in the stronger wind as long as possible.

If the gradient wind is less than about 10 knots the bands tend to deform, and sometimes large (5 to 10 miles across) eddies appear in the wind. These 'holes' move down the gradient wind, so if you get into one the best way to get out is to make way towards the gradient wind direction.

CHANGES IN WATER TEMPERATURE

A sudden change in water temperature of a few degrees is almost as significant as a coastline in influencing the wind. Over colder water the surface air will be cooled and become more stable, there will therefore be less vertical mixing and friction will cause the wind to back and slow down. Over warmer water the surface air will be warmed and become less stable, there will be more vertical mixing and

Figure 13.1

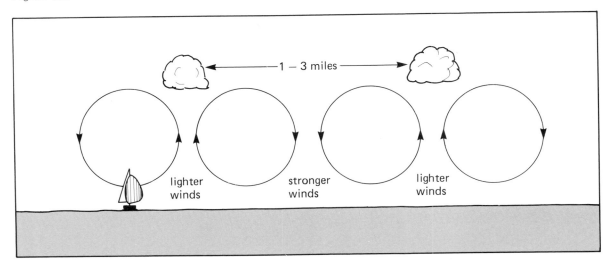

the effect of friction will be more readily overcome, so the wind will be stronger and more veered.

The zone or dividing line between cold and warm water will act as a 'coastline'. There will be a bend as the air moves from one to the other, the bend always on the side downwind of the transition. For winds blowing along the transition a zone of convergence and stronger winds – or divergence and lighter winds – will be found, depending upon the direction; also the wind will be generally stronger over the warmer water than over the cold.

It is not uncommon to find water temperature changes of 4 to 5 degrees C, particularly near estuaries or where there are large areas of tidal upwelling.

If the stability of the air is critical (i.e. the air is stable to the temperature over one area of water and unstable to the temperature of the adjacent area) the differences in wind speed between the two areas could be as high as 25 per cent, but the areas must be several miles across to be fully effective.

Across the Gulf Stream you can expect dramatic changes in wind speed in only a few miles as the water temperature changes – typically from 10 knots over the cold water to 20 to 25 knots over the adjacent warm water.

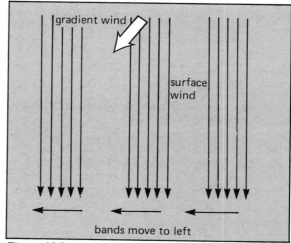

Figure 13.2

14 Looking for wind

If you are totally becalmed there is clearly nothing you can do to look for wind, you just have more time to study the weather. So make the most of it. The following are some of the things to think about.

• If you are within a few miles of the coast, will there be a sea breeze (by day) or land breeze (by night)? Or are you very temporarily in the calm zone associated with a developing sea breeze?

• If you are many miles from land, a falling barometer, increasing high cloud and increasing swell all tell of deteriorating weather and probably wind quite soon.

• A line of low cloud (probably stratocumulus) moving slowly towards you will herald a gentle breeze from a direction to the left of the direction of approach.

• A change of tide sometimes brings a little wind because it changes the direction of drag on the air, or draws in some warmer water.

If you have a little wind and want more, there are several possible courses of action.

1 If you are in the open sea and the forecast suggests that you should be in a stronger wind, and your own weather maps support this, then it is probable that you are caught in a light-wind band. So sail towards the band of stronger wind. This means making port tack until the wind has increased and then tacking onto starboard so as to stay as long as possible in the stronger wind.

2 If you are near the coast, try to work out from your knowledge of the coastal effects and of sea and land breezes where the stronger wind will be. For instance, if the wind is blowing along the coast and the land is on your right (back to wind) there will always be more wind (except for the sea breeze calm zone) within about three to five miles of the coast (or within about three miles of a line linking headlands if the coastline is wavy). If the land is on your left, stand well off except when a sea breeze is likely.

3 Water temperature is very important when the wind is light, and what wind there is will tend to keep to the zones of warmer water. In winter and spring try to avoid the colder coastal waters. In summer, tidal upwelling gives the coldest water but considerable local experience is necessary to judge where it is.

15 Weather hazards

What is that black cloud to windward – does it indicate a squall, a gale, a thunderstorm, fog, or is it just a patch of dirty, smoke-laden air? There are a number of questions you can ask which will at least help toward an answer, and may rule out some hazards, as follows:

- What was the latest weather forecast?
- What is the barometer doing?
- Has the wind changed in the last hour or two (speed and direction)?
- Have the waves changed? Is there any swell?
- What have the higher clouds been doing? Have they been typical of those ahead of a front or trough? Did you notice which way they were moving?
- Are you within ten miles of land?

All this information you should have in your log. It is important to refer to the *facts*, not your crew's ideas or hunches as to what may have happened recently.

GALES

Gales which are due to depressions (squalls are very short-lived in comparison and are considered separately) do not spring up without warning and with information in your log which will enable you to answer the above questions you will never be caught unawares. Watch out in particular for:

1 The weather forecast. If the possibility of a gale has been mentioned keep a listening watch on Radio 4 or the nearest coast radio station.

2 Your barometer. A fall of pressure of over 8 mb in three hours is almost certain to be followed by a gale whatever the wind is to start with, and a fall of over 5 mb in three hours by a force 6. If the wind is already force 7 you must expect a gale within an hour, but if it is only force 3 when your barometer starts falling at this rate you have at least four hours before the gale arrives. A very rapid rise in pressure after a trough has passed is also indicative of a gale, and the same rates of pressure change apply – a rise of over 6 mb in three hours for a force 8 and over 5 mb in three hours for a force 6. (You must make allowances for your own movement, either towards or away from the low pressure – Buys Ballot's law will tell you which

way you are going relative to the pressure centre.)

These rapid pressure changes are certain signs of a gale. They were in the 1979 Fastnet Race, when virtually all other signs were missing. But don't assume that because the barometer is not falling rapidly a gale is impossible. It will take longer to arrive, but all the other signs are important as well.

3 If the wind is backing and increasing at the same time it indicates a trough approaching, and you should find that the barometer is falling as well. If the black cloud of the trough is almost upon you the signs are of a temporary squall rather than a prolonged gale.

4 Waves on the sea produced by the local wind tell you no more than the wind itself, but swell waves can be a useful predictor. If they are increasing from the direction in which you know there is a depression an increase in wind is likely. Since swell waves take a long time to generate they usually indicate the approach of a large area of stronger winds which are likely to last for days rather than hours. There were no warning swell waves ahead of the 1979 Fastnet storm because the storm only developed as the first boats were approaching the Fastnet Rock.

5 High clouds increasing from the direction of lower pressure and travelling from a direction well veered on the surface wind (e.g. southerly surface wind and northwesterly upper wind) are a sign of increasing wind. The faster the high clouds are travelling the greater the likely increase in surface wind during the next six to twelve hours.

6 If the wind is blowing approximately along the coast so that with your back to the wind the coast is on your right-hand side, a force 6 to 7 wind either in harbour or 8 or more miles off the coast means a gale force 8 in a band within about 5 or 6 miles of the coast.

SQUALLS

Two different types of squall are met in practice, one due to thunderstorms which we deal with below, and one associated with either a cold front or a trough of low pressure in relatively cold air. Typically some miles ahead of such a trough you may be able to see a line of towering cumulus clouds, and along the line of the trough itself the clouds are dense and black with patches of heavy rain. Absence of swell waves, only a slow fall in pressure and no preceding increase in high cloud moving from a well veered direction all suggest a very temporary squall lasting not more than about half an hour, if that. The best advice is to reef and make for the lightest part of the cloud. Having weathered the squall you can usually assume that another one is unlikely for four to six hours.

THUNDERSTORMS

The dark mass of threatening cloud associated with a mature thunderstorm is often heralded by a decrease in wind and an almost glassy sea. These features clearly distinguish it from a depression or trough. The barometer may move up and down quite quickly and erratically by one or two millibars, but again the absence of a longer period fall distinguishes this from an approaching depression. The best rule to avoid the worst of the wind is to leave the storm to port. Squalls associated with the storm usually move steadily outwards from the centre with the wind ahead of them in the opposite direction, that is blowing in towards the storm.

Near the coast thunderstorms are more likely in the afternoon and early evening when land temperatures are at a maximum. Over the open ocean thunderstorm frequency is highest at night when cloud-top temperatures are at their lowest. As we saw in Chapter 1, this creates conditions of minimum stability over the sea.

For safety from lightning remember that tall, free-standing objects tend to be focal points for the electrical discharge to earth. So make sure that the conducting route (metal) through to the water is continuous. The crew are safe sitting well away from mast and shrouds.

FOG

Two main types of fog are met at sea: fog which has formed over land on a cool, clear night and drifted out over the water; and sea fog which forms over the sea itself when relatively warm moist air moves over colder water.

Drifting patches of land fog tend to lift to 3 to 6 metres or so above the sea surface and gradually break up as they move away from the coast. The warmer the water compared to the temperature of the air over the land, the quicker the fog disperses. So if you are in fog in harbour and the forecast is for fog over land clearing during the morning, you can safely sail out to sea expecting the fog to be gone by the time you return to port.

Satellite picture showing an area of sea fog moving around the north of Scotland.

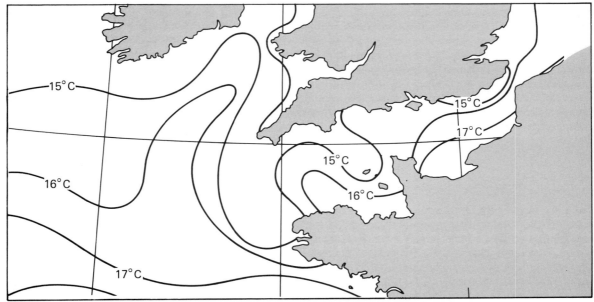

Figure 15.1

Sea fog

Sea fog forms typically in tropical maritime air as it moves northwards over colder waters. Expect it for instance in warm, moist southwesterly winds blowing in from the Azores or further south. The critical factors are the dewpoint of the air and the temperature of the sea surface.

The dewpoint of any particular mass of air is defined as the temperature to which it must be cooled for condensation to occur, that is for fog to form. Air from warm sea areas to the southwest arrives with a high dewpoint, often higher than the sea surface temperature around Britain, so it becomes characteristically foggy. Air originating over dry land or cold seas has a low dewpoint, usually well below the sea surface temperature around Britain and is not associated with fog.

When the dewpoint value is marginal the incidence of fog relates to the variation in sea temperature. In winter and spring the sea is coldest inshore so fog forms more frequently inshore than out to sea. In summer and autumn the sea is coldest away from the shore so fog forms more frequently out to sea. There are always variations in sea temperature from place to place, and consequently variations in sea fog. Many changes in sea temperature are due to the tide, so the position and extent of fog banks alter with changes in the tide.

If the dewpoint of the air is everywhere well above the sea temperature, widespread or extensive fog is forecast. If it is only a little above sea temperature, and in some cases may not be so, fog banks are forecast. If the dewpoint of the air is above the sea temperature only in a few places fog patches are forecast, and coastal fog in winter and spring.

If you are caught in widespread fog there is little you can do other than sail to the lee of the nearest land or wait for the next cold front.

The sample of sea surface temperature isotherms for a typical five-day period in July (figure 15.1) illustrates how variable the temperature is. If the dewpoint of air moving in on southwesterly winds was 15 degrees C, fog would be widespread south of Cornwall and in the Bristol Channel, but the coastal waters off northern France would be largely clear.

As a sea fog gets older its characteristics gradually change: it becomes colder and heavier, and immune to variations in sea temperature. The 'haar' which sometimes envelopes the coasts of north and east Scotland is of this type. It starts life in warm, moist southerly winds moving over colder seas around Ireland. By the time it reaches Scotland a day or more later it has cooled many degrees (by radiation from the top of the fog) and becomes a very wet and persistent fog with few if any breaks except in the lee of the land.

16 Wind and tide

Changes in the tidal streams influence the wind in three ways:
- Through change in drag on the wind.
- Through changes in water temperature.
- Through changes in the temperature of the shore.

Change in drag on the wind

This effect is easy to appreciate. When the tide is running with the wind the drag of the water on the wind is less than normal for a given wind strength, particularly since the sea would be relatively smooth and the length of waves relatively long. A tidal stream running against the wind involves a considerable increase in drag, due both to the change in relative speed and the increase in height and steepness of the waves. The actual windspeed then decreases and the direction backs a few degrees.

Change in water temperature

A change in tide is often accompanied by a change in water temperature, up or down depending upon whether the ebb or flood is from a warmer or colder source, or as a consequence of upwelling of colder water from beneath. Colder water leads to colder air near the sea surface, and thus increased stability and a lighter, more backed wind at the sea surface for a given pressure gradient wind. Warmer water leads to warmer air near the sea surface, decreased stability and a stronger, more veered wind for a given pressure gradient.

So the clear message is: if you want the stronger and more veered wind, sail in the warmer water; if you want the lighter and more backed wind, sail in the colder water.

Change in shore temperature

The flooding by cold water of large areas of sun-heated mudflats or sand changes significantly (and often suddenly) the local sea-breeze generating forces. Consequent changes in wind speed and direction can be expected within two or three miles of the shore.

17 Waves and swell

There are two different types of waves: wind waves, which are produced locally by the wind blowing at the time, and swell waves, which are generated by the wind somewhere else. The 'somewhere else' can be thousands of miles away. The height and distance apart of waves depends on:
- The strength of the wind.
- The length of time it has been blowing.
- The fetch, which is the distance the wind has been blowing over the water.
- The depth of water.
- In the case of swell: the distance the waves have travelled.

Wind waves

Locally produced wind waves are generated very quickly, within an hour or so, and provided the wind is steady, the longer it blows the longer the wave length becomes. The wave front will often lie at an angle of a few degrees to the left of the wind direc-tion, which will tend to make port tack a little faster than starboard. If the wind direction is changing, as with a sea breeze for instance, this angle between the wind and the wave front may be quite large. On the passage of a trough or front there will often be two distinct sets of waves, the angle between them being the difference in wind angles either side of the trough. In the 1979 Fastnet storm the wave length was short both ahead of and behind the cold front, because the wind, though very strong, had been blowing for only a few hours. The resulting sea was notably confused.

The time taken for wind waves to decay depends on how long the wind that produced them was blow-ing. A fair rule of thumb is that the generation and decay times are similar.

If the wind is against the tide the wave length shortens, while it increases if the tide and wind are in the same direction. A strong current opposing a strong wind produces very steep and potentially

dangerous waves especially in tidal races near headlands. Wind and tide in the same direction increase the wave length considerably and make for much easier sailing.

Swell waves

The important swell waves are those that are generated over vast areas of open ocean. They contain a great deal of energy and take a long time (days) to decay. Swell waves always become steeper as they approach a shore, when the depth of water becomes less than one-twentieth of the wave length. This happens for wind waves as well, but not in water of sailing depth.

It is a useful fact that the longer swell waves travel faster than the shorter wind waves, so they can travel ahead and give advance warning of an approaching depression. Therefore the arrival or absence of swell provides a clear distinction between the advance of a local thunderstorm and an approaching deep depression. A threatening sky with increasing black clouds and rain cannot be part of an existing large wind system if there is no swell propagating forwards

from it, so any wind will be temporary. On the other hand, increasing swell from the direction of advance of the storm clouds suggests an approaching depression with a large area of strong winds coming your way.

If there is swell which has been present for a long time without significant change the interpretation is doubtful: for instance the depression may be advancing, but very slowly.

Freak waves

There really is no such thing as a freak wave. So many waves are generated in the sea and are continually combining together to form different sized waves, that statistically some are always bigger than others. The seventh wave is popularly supposed to be bigger than the other six. Similarly, there is the one in a hundred bigger still, the one in a thousand even bigger, and so on. Whether you sail the Channel, the Bay of Biscay or the Atlantic you must expect to experience a wave bigger than the rest. The risk of being pooped or knocked onto your beam is always there, so be prepared.

18 Examples

1 WHERE TO ANCHOR FOR LUNCH?

You have a day off. The tide is right for a day's sail starting early at about 0730. Your coast faces approximately east, and there are some pleasant coves and a couple of small islands.

The shipping forecast indicates wind southwest force 3-4 with nothing said about it increasing or decreasing, and fair weather. Most coastal stations report for 0400 pressure 'falling slowly' or 'now falling', but the pressure is little different from that of the previous day, so the slowly falling pressure is nothing to worry about – the change is only diurnal. You notice a few clouds moving across from the southwest, which confirms the gradient wind inferred from the forecast. It is in quadrant one, and since you expect a fairly sunny day a good sea breeze is certain: starting fairly early from the east, slowly veering to SSE and probably not dying away till towards evening. So you decide that setting a course NNE would end up with a long, hard beat back to port. Instead you set course to the SE, making for the northwest-facing

bay of a small island eight miles away. This will give a good anchorage for lunch, shelter from both the sea breeze and the sea-breeze chop, and confidence of a good wind home.

2 RACE OFFICER

You are selected for committee boat duty for a race in Poole Bay. The shipping forecast is for a southwesterly wind force 3-4. Observations at 0400 from Channel Light Vessel and Scilly show pressure rising slowly with southwest winds force 4 at both positions. As you look out at Lymington at 0700 it is cloudy and the wind appears to be in the west. The land area forecast, however, is for a fairly sunny day.

Arriving in the course area at 1000 you find a 12-knot wind of 210 degrees. The gradient wind is in quadrant three so there will be no sea breeze. The slowly rising pressure suggests a ridge moving in and perhaps a slackening and veering wind, but the expectation of a sunny day suggests a tendency for pressure to fall as the land warms up, possibly strengthening and marginally backing the gradient. So you do not waste any time and lay the windward mark on a bearing of 210 degrees.

3 ACROSS THE CHANNEL AND BACK

Your weekend in Alderney has been planned for several weeks. You have studied the tides and decided on the best ETD to give you a favourable tide out of the Solent. Ideally you would like a wind on the beam for a fast reach both ways; for a crossing from the Needles this means either a northwesterly or a southeasterly. But as so often happens there is a seemingly endless sequence of depressions moving northeast between Scotland and Iceland, with their attendant fronts and intervening ridges moving east through the Channel.

On the Monday before you sail the Marinecall 5-day forecast indicates the probability of a southerly, and you prepare yourself for a beat all the way, thankful that the strength is only 4 to 5. You follow the weather maps in the daily papers all week, and on Friday you use the 1355 shipping bulletin to produce a more detailed map (figure 18.1). This bears out the earlier indications. The forecast for sea area Wight is 'south to southwest 4 to 5 occasionally 6'. Referring to the map it is clear that the forecast direction – south to southwest – means southwesterly to start with, backing southerly as the warm front approaches, then veering southwesterly behind it. Judging from the distance apart of the isobars it looks as though the wind will be strongest just ahead of the front – which is where the 'occasionally force 6' comes in.

The spacing of the isobars along the warm front gives a warm front speed of about 15 knots, from which you deduce that it will be crossing Alderney at about mid-day on Saturday. So, realising that you will have a beat all the way, you decide to use the wind changes to advantage by leaving the Needles on starboard tack while the wind is southwesterly and going about on to port as it backs towards southerly. You hope to make sufficient way to weather

of Alderney to be able to close the island on starboard after the warm front has passed. You pay constant attention to the forecasts and to your barometer or barograph in case of unforeseen changes. The one remaining problem is the visibility and the probability of fog in the warm sector (between the warm and cold fronts).

The return trip on Sunday will be in the ridge behind the cold front (figure 18.2). The forecast is northwesterly 2 to 3 with good visibility. The weather map indicates a gradual backing in the wind, so you will be sailing freer as you cross. Closing the English coast after dusk will be complicated by the remains of the afternoon sea breeze – a calm patch, perhaps, and maybe an hour or two of southwesterly wind (see Chapter 12), details which are never included in a shipping bulletin. With the forecast northwesterly gradient wind the night wind in the Solent is likely to be strongest near the island shore, whereas the afternoon sea breeze (southwesterly) will be strongest near the mainland shore.

Figure 18.1

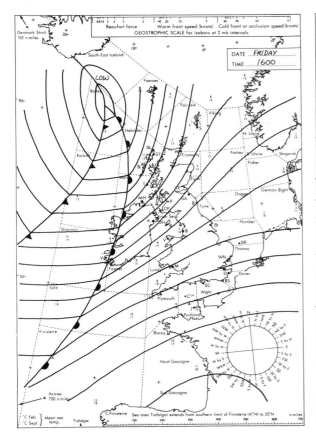

Figure 18.2

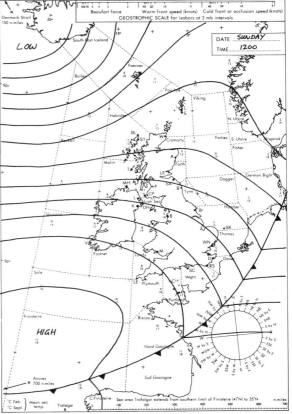

The following examples show how to transcribe and use the shipping bulletins described in Chapter 9.

AND NOW THE SHIPPING FORECAST ISSUED BY THE METEOROLOGICAL OFFICE AT 1705 ON SUNDAY 27TH MARCH

GALE WARNINGS ARE IN OPERATION FOR SEA AREAS FINISTERRE, SOLE, AND ROCKALL

THE GENERAL SYNOPSIS AT 1200
LOW FINISTERRE 996 MOVING NORTHEAST TO SOUTH NORWAY 995 BY THE SAME TIME TOMORROW. LOW HEBRIDES 995 EXPECTED 400 MILES NORTH OF VIKING 978 BY THE SAME TIME

THE AREA FORECASTS FOR THE NEXT 24 HOURS
VIKING, NORTH UTSIRE, SOUTH UTSIRE, FORTIES
SOUTHERLY VEERING WESTERLY 5 TO 6, RAIN MOVING EAST THEN SHOWERS, MODERATE WITH FOG PATCHES BECOMING GOOD
CROMARTY, FORTH
SOUTHERLY 4 TO 5 VEERING WESTERLY AND INCREASING 7, RAIN THEN SHOWERS, MODERATE OR POOR BECOMING GOOD
TYNE, DOGGER, FISHER, GERMAN BIGHT
SOUTHERLY 5 TO 7 VEERING NORTHWEST LATER, RAIN LATER, MODERATE WITH FOG PATCHES BECOMING GOOD
HUMBER, THAMES, DOVER
SOUTHERLY 4 TO 5 VEERING NORTHWEST 7, RAIN LATER, MODERATE OR GOOD BUT POOR FOR A TIME
WIGHT, PORTLAND, PLYMOUTH
SOUTHERLY VEERING NORTHWESTERLY 4 TO 5 INCREASING 7 FOR A TIME, RAIN OR SHOWERS BECOMING FAIR, GOOD BUT POOR FOR A TIME
BISCAY
SOUTHEASTERLY BECOMING NORTHERLY, 4 TO 5 INCREASING 7, RAIN AT TIMES, MODERATE LOCALLY POOR AT FIRST
FINISTERRE, SOLE
NORTHWEST 6 TO 8 BUT SOUTHERLY 5 TO 7 IN EAST AT FIRST, RAIN AT TIMES, MODERATE OR POOR
LUNDY, FASTNET, IRISH SEA
SOUTHERLY VEERING NORTHWESTERLY 4 TO 5 BUT INCREASING 7 FOR A TIME, RAIN THEN FAIR, MODERATE OCCASIONALLY POOR BECOMING GOOD
SHANNON
NORTHWEST 5 BECOMING SOUTHERLY 6 TO GALE 8, SHOWERS THEN RAIN, GOOD BECOMING MODERATE
ROCKALL
WEST 6 INCREASING GALE 8 FOR A TIME BACKING SOUTHERLY LATER, SHOWERS, MAINLY GOOD
MALIN, HEBRIDES, BAILEY, FAIR ISLE
SOUTHWEST 5 VEERING WESTERLY 6 TO GALE 8, RAIN THEN SHOWERS, MODERATE OR POOR BECOMING GOOD
FAEROES
CYCLONIC 5 BECOMING WESTERLY 5 TO 7, SHOWERS, MODERATE BECOMING GOOD
SOUTHEAST ICELAND
CYCLONIC 4 BECOMING NORTHWEST 5, RAIN OR SHOWERS, GOOD

WEATHER REPORTS FROM COASTAL STATIONS FOR 1600
TIREE
WEST FOUR, 19 MILES, 1002, RISING
BUTT OF LEWIS
SOUTH SOUTH WEST, INTERMITTENT SLIGHT RAIN, 11 MILES, 997, FALLING MORE SLOWLY
SUMBURGH
SOUTH SOUTH EAST 4, HAZE, 2 MILES, 1001, FALLING
ST ABBS HEAD
SOUTHWEST 5, HAZE, 2 MILES, 1004, NOW RISING
SMITHS KNOLL AUTOMATIC
SOUTHEAST 3, 5 MILES, 1008, STEADY
DOVER
SOUTHWEST 3, 5 MILES, 1008, FALLING SLOWLY
ROYAL SOVEREIGN
SOUTHWEST BY SOUTH 4, 5 MILES, 1008, FALLING SLOWLY
CHANNEL LIGHT VESSEL AUTOMATIC
SOUTHWEST 1, 11 MILES, 1007, RISING SLOWLY
LANDS END
EAST SOUTH EAST 4, MIST, 1 MILE, 1005, FALLING
VALENTIA
NORTH 3, INTERMITTENT SLIGHT RAIN, 6 MILES, 1006, RISING SLOWLY
RONALDSWAY
SOUTH BY WEST 4, SMOKE, 3 MILES, 1005, NOW FALLING
MALIN HEAD
WEST BY SOUTH 4, INTERMITTENT SLIGHT RAIN, 16 MILES, 1003, RISING
JERSEY
SOUTHEAST BY SOUTH 3, 16 MILES, 1007, FALLING MORE SLOWLY."

R. MET. SOC./R.Y.A. METMAP

GENERAL SYNOPSIS   at ...1200......... ~~GMT~~/BST ...27 MARCH...

L   Fin → NE   S Nor 995
L   Heb → 400 m N of Vik 978

Gales	SEA AREA FORECAST		Wind	Weather	Visibility
	Viking	⎫			
	N. Utsire	⎬	S/W 5-6	• → E/▽	m ≡ / g
	S. Utsire				
	Forties	⎭			
	Cromarty	⎫	S 4-5/W7	• | ▽	m p / g
	Forth	⎬			
	Tyne	⎭			
	Dogger	⎫	S 5-7/NW	|•	m ≡ / g
	Fisher	⎬			
	German Bight	⎭			
	Humber	⎫			
	Thames	⎬	S 4-5/NW7	|•	m/g |p|
	Dover	⎭			
	Wight	⎫			
	Portland	⎬	S/NW 4-5 → |7|	• or ▽/f	g |p|
	Plymouth	⎭			
	Biscay	—	SE/N 4-5/7	•	m loc p|
	~~Trafalgar~~				
X	Finisterre	⎫	NW 6-8 S 5-7 in E/	•	m/p
X	Sole	⎬			
	Lundy	⎫			
	Fastnet	⎬	S/NW 4-5 |7|	• |f	m occ p/g
	Irish Sea	⎭			
	Shannon	—	NW 5/S 6-8	▽ |•	g/m
X	Rockall	—	W 6/8 |5	▽	mg
	Malin	⎫			
	Hebrides	⎬	SW 5/W 6-8	• |▽	mp/g
	Bailey	⎭			
	Fair Isle	⎫			
	Faeroes	—	cyc 5/ W 5-7	▽	m/g
	SE Iceland	—	cyc 4/ NW 5	• ▽	g

COASTAL REPORTS (Shipping Bulletin) at ..1600.. BST ~~GMT~~	Direction	Force	Weather	Visibility	Pressure	Trend
	Wind					
Tiree	W	4		19	02	r
Butt of Lewis	SSW	6	•	11	97	fms
Sumburgh	SSE	4	h	2	01	f
St Abb's Head	SW	5	h	2	04	nr
Smiths Knoll Auto	SE	3		5	08	s
Dover	SW	3		5	08	fs
Royal Sovereign	SW/S	4		5	08	fs
Channel L.V. Auto	SW	1		11	07	rs
Land's End	ESE	4	m	1	05	f
Valentia	N	3	•	6	06	rs
Ronaldsway	S/W	4	s	3	05	nf
Malin Head	W/S	4	•	16	03	r
Jersey	SE/S	3		16	07	fms

COASTAL REPORTS (Inshore Waters) at .... BST/GMT					
Boulmer					
Bridlington					
Walton on the Naze					
St Catherine's Point					
Land's End					
Mumbles					
Valley					
Blackpool					
Ronaldsway					
Killough					
Orlock Head					
Larne					
Corsewall Point					
Prestwick					
Benbecula					
Stornoway					
Lerwick					
Wick					
Aberdeen					
Leuchars					

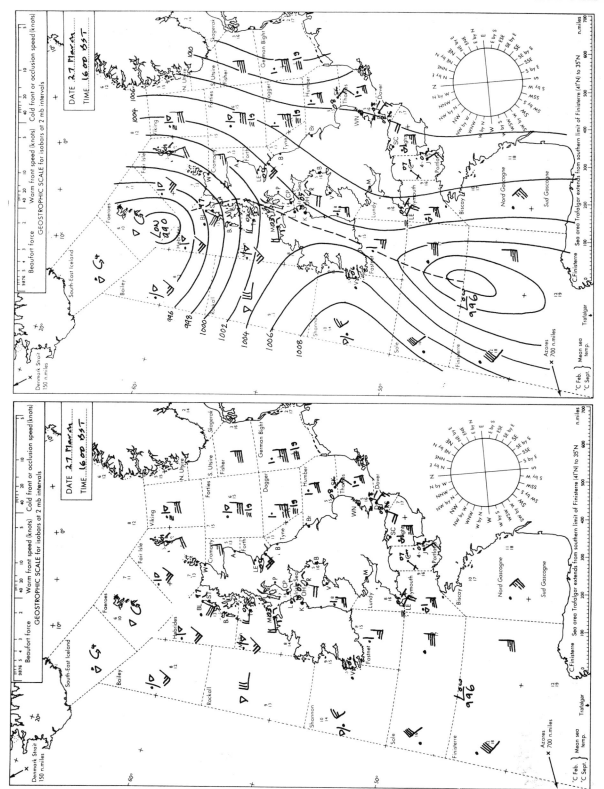

"AND NOW THE SHIPPING FORECAST ISSUED BY THE METEOROLOGICAL OFFICE AT 1705 ON MONDAY 28TH MARCH

GALE WARNINGS ARE IN OPERATION FOR SEA AREAS FINISTERRE, SOLE, SHANNON, ROCKALL, MALIN, HEBRIDES, BAILEY, FAIR ISLE, SOUTHEAST ICELAND

THE GENERAL SYNOPSIS AT 1200
ATLANTIC LOW MOVING NORTHEAST EXPECTED 200 MILES WEST OF ROCKALL 978 BY SAME TIME TOMORROW

THE AREA FORECASTS FOR THE NEXT 24 HOURS
VIKING
WEST 5 BACKING SOUTH AND INCREASING 6 TO GALE 8, SHOWERS, MODERATE OR GOOD
NORTH UTSIRE, SOUTH UTSIRE
WEST BACKING SOUTH 4 TO 5, SHOWERS, MODERATE OR GOOD
FORTIES, CROMARTY, FORTH
WEST BACKING SOUTH 4 TO 5 OCCASIONALLY 6, LOCALLY GALE 8 LATER. SHOWERS AT FIRST, MODERATE OR GOOD
TYNE, DOGGER
NORTHWESTERLY BACKING SOUTHERLY 4 TO 5, SHOWERS AT FIRST, MODERATE OR GOOD
FISHER, GERMAN BIGHT
WEST TO NORTHWEST 4 TO 5 BECOMING VARIABLE 3, SHOWERS AT FIRST, MODERATE BECOMING GOOD
HUMBER, THAMES
NORTHWESTERLY 5 BACKING SOUTHERLY AND DECREASING 3 TO 4, SHOWERS AT FIRST, MODERATE BECOMING GOOD
DOVER, WIGHT, PORTLAND
CYCLONIC 3 TO 4, SHOWERS, MODERATE OR GOOD
PLYMOUTH
NORTHERLY 5 TO 6 BACKING SOUTHWESTERLY AND DECREASING 3 TO 4, MAINLY FAIR, MODERATE OR GOOD
BISCAY
VARIABLE 3 BECOMING NORTHERLY 5 IN WEST, MAINLY FAIR, MODERATE OR GOOD
FINISTERRE
NORTHERLY 6 TO 7 LOCALLY GALE 8 AT FIRST DECREASING 5 LATER, MAINLY FAIR, GOOD
SOLE
NORTHERLY 6 TO GALE 8 BACKING SOUTHERLY AND DECREASING 5, RAIN AT TIMES, GOOD BECOMING MODERATE
LUNDY, FASTNET
NORTHERLY BACKING SOUTHWESTERLY 5 TO 6 DECREASING 4 FOR A TIME, MAINLY FAIR, MAINLY GOOD

IRISH SEA
NORTHERLY 4 BACKING SOUTH TO SOUTHWESTERLY INCREASING 5 TO 6, FAIR, MAINLY GOOD
SHANNON, ROCKALL
SOUTHERLY 5 INCREASING 6 TO GALE 8 OCCASIONALLY SEVERE GALE 9, RAIN OR SHOWERS, GOOD BECOMING MODERATE OR POOR
MALIN, HEBRIDES
WESTERLY 4 TO 5 LOCALLY 7 AT FIRST, BACKING SOUTHERLY AND INCREASING 6 TO GALE 8, RAIN LATER, GOOD BECOMING MODERATE
BAILEY
WESTERLY 4 TO 5 BACKING SOUTH TO SOUTHEASTERLY 6 TO GALE 8 OCCASIONALLY SEVERE GALE 9, RAIN LATER, GOOD BECOMING MODERATE
FAIR ISLE, FAEROES, SOUTH EAST ICELAND
WESTERLY 5 TO 7 DECREASING 4 THEN BACKING SOUTH TO SOUTHEASTERLY AND INCREASING GALE FORCE 8, SHOWERS AT FIRST THEN RAIN, GOOD BECOMING MODERATE

WEATHER REPORTS FROM COASTAL STATIONS FOR 1600
TIREE
WEST BY NORTH FIVE, 27 MILES, 1015, RISING
BUTT OF LEWIS
WEST BY SOUTH SEVEN, PRECIPITATION WITHIN SIGHT, 11 MILES, 1010 RISING
SUMBURGH
WESTSOUTHWEST FIVE, PRECIPITATION WITHIN SIGHT, 19 MILES, 1005, RISING MORE SLOWLY
ST ABBS HEAD
WEST BY NORTH SIX, 22 MILES, 1014, RISING
SMITHS KNOLL AUTOMATIC
NORTH SIX, 11 MILES, 1012, RISING
DOVER
WESTSOUTHWEST TWO, 5 MILES, 1013, RISING
ROYAL SOVEREIGN
SOUTHWEST FOUR, 5 MILES, 1014, RISING
CHANNEL LIGHT VESSEL AUTOMATIC
WESTNORTHWEST TWO, 5 MILES, 1015, RISING
LANDS END
NORTH BY EAST SEVEN, 13 MILES, 1016, RISING
VALENTIA
WEST BY NORTH THREE, 22 MILES, 1020, RISING MORE SLOWLY
RONALDSWAY
NORTHWEST BY WEST FOUR, MORE THAN 38 MILES, 1018, RISING MORE SLOWLY
MALIN HEAD
WEST FOUR, 22 MILES, 1017, RISING
JERSEY
WEST BY NORTH TWO, 7 MILES, 1015, RISING."

R. MET. SOC./R.Y.A. METMAP

GENERAL SYNOPSIS	at 1200 GMT/BST 28 MARCH
	Atl L → NE → 200 m W of R 978

Gales	SEA AREA FORECAST		Wind	Weather	Visibility
	Viking	⌐	WS | S 6-8	▽	m or g
	N. Utsire	⎰	W | S 4-5	▽	m or g
	S. Utsire	⎱			
	Forties	⎰			
	Cromarty	⎰	W | S 4-5 occ 6 | 8	▽ |	m g
	Forth	⎱			
	Tyne	⎰	NW | S 4-5	▽ |	mg
	Dogger	⎱			
	Fisher	⎰	W – NW 4-5 | V 3	▽ |	m | g
	German Bight	⎱			
	Humber	⎰	NWS | S 3-4	▽ |	m | g
	Thames	⎱			
	Dover	⎰			
	Wight	⎱	Cyc 3-4	▽	mg
	Portland	⎱			
	Plymouth	—	N 5-6 | SW 3-4	mf	mg
	Biscay	—	V 3 | N in W	mf	mg
	~~Trafalgar~~				
X	Finisterre	—	N 6-7 loc 8 | S	mf	g
X	Sole	—	N 6-8 | S 5	•	g | m
	Lundy	⎰	N | SW 5-6 | 4 |	mf	mg
	Fastnet	⎱			
	Irish Sea	—	N4 | S-SW 5-6	f	mg
X	Shannon	⎰	S 5 | 6-8 occ 9	• ▽	g | m p
X	Rockall	⎱			
X	Malin	⎰	W 4-5 loc 7 | S 6-8	| •	g | m
X	Hebrides	⎱			
X	Bailey	—	W 4-5 | S-SE 6-8 occ 9	| •	g | m
X	Fair Isle	⎰			
	Faeroes	⎰	W 5-7 | 4 | S-SE 8	▽ | •	g | m
X	SE Iceland	⎱			

COASTAL REPORTS (Shipping Bulletin) at 1600 BST GMT	Wind Direction	Force	Weather	Visibility	Pressure	Trend
Tiree	W/N	5		27	15	r
Butt of Lewis	W/S	7	☽	11	10	r
Sumburgh	WSW	5	☽	19	05	rms
St Abb's Head	W/N	6		22	14	r
Smiths Knoll Auto	N	6		11	12	r
Dover	WSW	2		5	13	r
Royal Sovereign	SW	4		5	14	r
Channel L.V. Auto	WNW	2		5	15	r
Land's End	N/E	7		13	16	r
Valentia	N/N	3		22	20	rms
Ronaldsway	NW/W	4		>38	18	rms
Malin Head	W	4		22	17	r
Jersey	N/N	2		7	15	r

7/90

COASTAL REPORTS (Inshore Waters) at .... BST/GMT						
Boulmer						
Bridlington						
Walton on the Naze						
St Catherine's Point						
Land's End						
Mumbles						
Valley						
Blackpool						
Ronaldsway						
Killough						
Orlock Head						
Larne						
Corsewall Point						
Prestwick						
Benbecula						
Stornoway						
Lerwick						
Wick						
Aberdeen						
Leuchars						

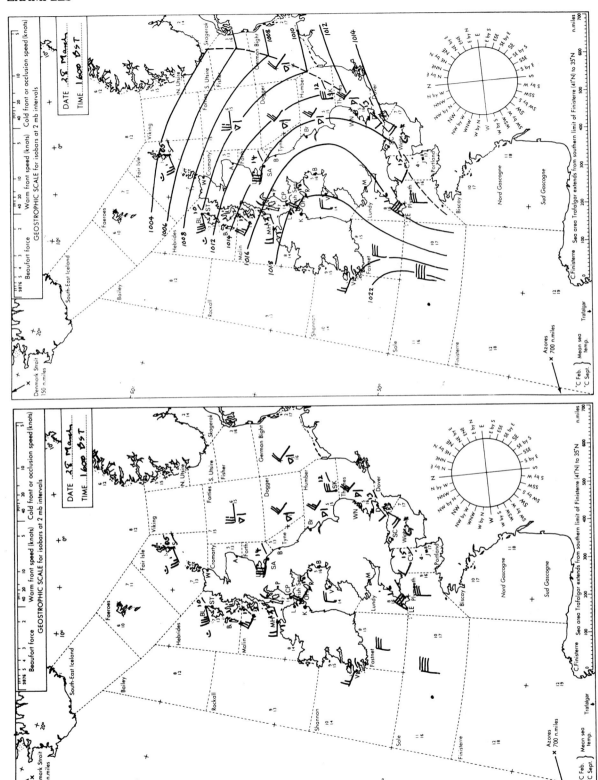

19 Mariner's weather lore

Much mariner's weather lore is useful and relates to the more frequently experienced sequences of wind, weather, cloud, and pressure changes.

> When the wind backs and the weather glass falls,
> Then be on your guard against gales and squalls.

combines the signs of falling pressure and backing wind to provide a very reliable indication of the strong winds of an approaching depression. Looking at a backing wind only, the saying:

> When the wind goes against the sun,
> Trust it not for back 'twill run.

provides only a note of caution.

The following saying is a good guide to the hurricane season in the Caribbean:

> June – too soon;
> July – stand by;
> August – look out you must;
> September – remember;
> October – all over.

The following three sayings feature the sort of high clouds which typically precede a warm front or the trough of an approaching depression – particularly the long hair-like trails of cirrus, and sometimes cirrocumulus and altocumulus with its characteristic cellular structure.

> If clouds look as if scratched by a hen,
> Get ready to reef your topsails then.

> Trace in the sky the painter's brush,
> Then winds around you soon will rush.

> Mackerel sky and mare's tails,
> Make lofty ships carry low sails.

There are rules of thumb associated with the barometer:

> When the glass falls low,
> Prepare for a blow;
> When it rises high,
> Let all your kites fly.

is so obvious that it needs no further explanation. But two others related to pressure changes deserve comment:

> First rise after low,
> foretells stronger blow.

describes what happens following some of the more vigorous cold fronts, when it is not unusual for the rise in pressure as the colder heavier air sweeps in to be so rapid that the pressure gradient increases dramatically. As a result the wind rises by two or three Beaufort forces for an hour or two.

> Long foretold, long last,
> Short notice soon past.

relates to the fact that major changes in the weather pattern are often preceded by several days of either falling or rising pressure, whereas rapid variations in pressure are characteristic of frequent and often rapid changes in the weather.

The ancient saying attributed to Virgil,

> For ere the rising winds begin to roar,
> The working seas advance to wash the shore.

is remarkable for its perception. In Chapter 17 we saw how swell waves travel relatively quickly and often give advance warning of an approaching depression with its strong winds.

> Rain before seven,
> fine before eleven.

merely highlights the fact that rain rarely lasts more than four hours at a time. It could equally read 'rain before eight, fine before twelve', or any other period of four hours in the day.

> Sky red in the morning,
> Is a sailor's sure warning;
> Sky red at night,
> Is the sailor's delight.

is the sailor's version of the well-known shepherd's saying. It works on something like 60 per cent of occasions of a red sky, and is based on the observed sequence of events when the weather is moving from west to east – as is often the case. A red sky is seen in the morning when the rising sun illuminates cloud moving in from the west, typically with a front approaching. A red sky is seen in the evening when the setting sun illuminates cloud which is moving away eastwards followed by clearer weather from the west.

The following two sayings relate to the haloes which appear around the moon when it shines through a thin veil of cirrostratus, cloud which often precedes a warm front or trough; hence the reference to increasing wind.

If on her cheeks you see the maiden's blush,
The ruddy moon foreshows that winds will rush.

Weather foul expect when thou canst trace
A baleful halo circling Phoebus' face.

Another rhyme is worth remembering if only to scotch the often paraded idea that the moon is somehow responsible for changes in the weather. It is not. The reason for the misconception is the frequent change which both display, and the inevitable coincidences that arise.

The moon and the weather
May change together,
But change of the moon
Does not change the weather.
If we'd no moon at all,
And that may seem strange,
We still would have weather
That's subject to change.

Appendix 1 Coriolis force

If you have a sailor's appreciation of basic navigation skills you should find the following non-mathematical explanation of Coriolis force fairly easy to grasp. The golf-ball analogy in Chapter 1 helps a little, but it does not explain why eastward and westward moving air is also subject to a deflection. So let us visualise a spinning globe, see what the effects of the spin are at the pole and the equator, and then interpolate for the mid-latitudes.

The earth is spinning on an axis that passes through the north and south poles. If a mass of polar air moves away from the pole, it must be deflected because of the spin, whatever direction it moves in. In practice air over the north pole can only move south, and air over the south pole can only move north. And as it does so it is subject to an increase in the movement of the earth's surface beneath it, like the golf ball. But this is only part of the story.

At the pole the spin axis is vertical to the earth's surface, which spins round it. The rate of spin is highest at this point, so Coriolis force is at a maximum. At the equator the spin axis is horizontal to the earth's surface, which moves around it like the rim of a wheel and does not spin at all – so the Coriolis force is zero.

Anywhere between the equator and the poles there will always be a component of the spin acting on moving air. It increases from zero at the equator to a maximum at the poles. This is the aspect most difficult to visualise. Try to imagine a three-dimensional spinning globe. If you stand a pencil over the pole it will be along the spin axis and you can visualise the pencil rotating and the earth spinning around it. Keeping the pencil vertical to the surface of the globe, slide it on its end until it reaches the equator. The component of spin about the axis of the pencil will gradually decrease until it becomes zero at the equator. It depends on the latitude. So wherever you are on the earth's surface – except at the equator – there is always a component of the earth's spin operating. The practical effect of this is to deflect sideways anything that moves freely – be it air or water, a golf ball or a bullet – and the deflection will operate regardless of the direction in which it is moving.

It is proverbially believed that bath water escaping down the plug hole is subject to Coriolis force and spins to the right in the northern hemisphere and to the left in the southern hemisphere. Not so! The fact is that for Coriolis force to be measurable the movement must cover a large area – a few kilometres at least – or last for an hour or two. The exit of the bath water is invariably determined by the way the plug is removed. Try it! Whether you are north or south of the equator you can get it spinning in either direction.

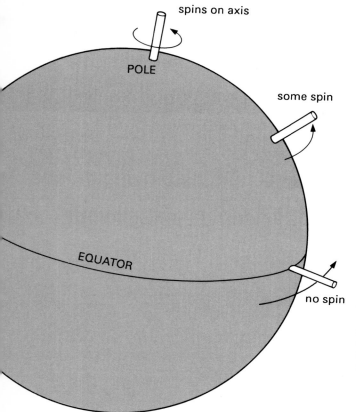

spins on axis

POLE

some spin

EQUATOR

no spin

Left: At the equator, an object on the earth's surface travels fast but does not spin. At the pole it stays in one place but spins on its axis. If the object (or air mass) is moved away from the equator towards the pole the rate of horizontal movement decreases but the spin increases.

Appendix 2 The thermal wind

Let us imagine vertical slices of warm and cold air some distance apart (figure A2.1), and assume that there is no pressure gradient at the ground and therefore no wind. Since pressure equates to weight, this means that the slice of warm air is the same weight as the slice of cold air.

Let us now go upwards through these slices to a typical height of altocumulus clouds, say 5000 metres. Since cold air is denser and therefore heavier for the same depth than warm air, the decrease in pressure through the cold air will be greater than the decrease through the warm air. So as we rise there will be a steadily increasing pressure difference between the two slices. By the time we reach 5000 metres this pressure difference may be enough to give a wind of typically 50 to 100 knots: a wind entirely due to the temperature difference between the two slices of air. This is known as the thermal wind.

When there is a pressure gradient – and therefore wind – at the ground to start with, the wind component arising from the temperature difference between the two slices will be superimposed on the surface wind. In other words the thermal wind is the vector difference between the wind at any two heights and is directly related to the average horizontal temperature gradient in the air between those heights. The greater the temperature difference the stronger the wind.

In practice, wherever you are on the earth there is nearly always a temperature difference from place to place as areas of warmer or colder air move around, so there is nearly always a thermal wind with clouds moving at different speeds and in different directions at different heights. Figure A2.2 is a chart of isotherms of mean temperature for the bottom 5500 metres of the atmosphere for a day in September. A chart of

Figure A2.1

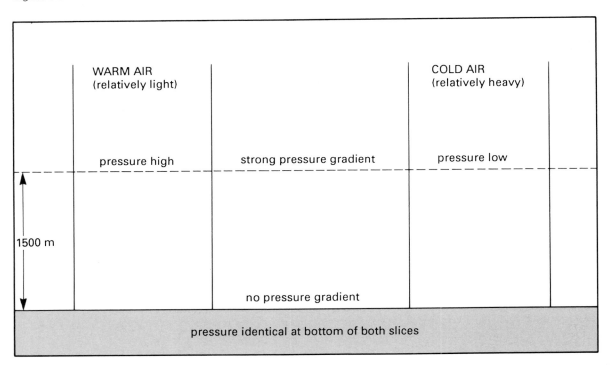

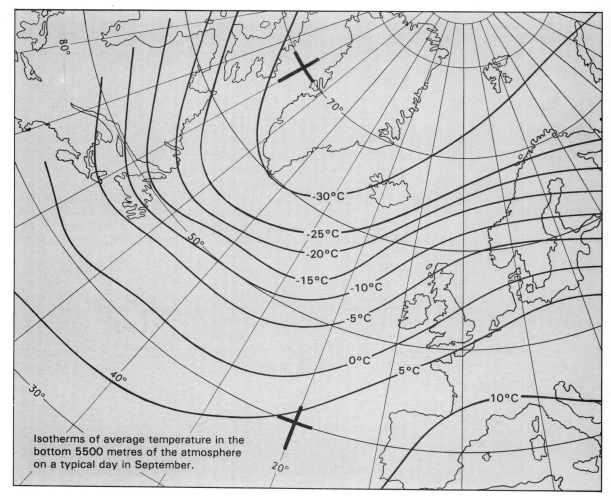

Isotherms of average temperature in the bottom 5500 metres of the atmosphere on a typical day in September.

Figure A2.2

the pressure difference between the surface and 5500 metres would have exactly the same shape, and the vector wind difference – which like all winds is subject to Coriolis force – will blow parallel to the isobars (or isotherms).

Most of this may seem very theoretical, but one helpful practical application is the thermal equivalent of Buys Ballot's Law which states that if you stand with your back to the thermal wind the lower temperature will be to your left and the higher temperature to your right. So ahead of a warm front advancing from the west the isotherms will lie from approximately northwest to southeast and the thermal wind will be northwesterly, with warm air to the west (figure A2.2). The surface wind is likely to be southerly, but the cirrus and altostratus clouds will

typically be seen streaming across from the northwest indicating a strong northwesterly thermal wind. The faster the clouds move the stronger the thermal wind and therefore the more vigorous the front is likely to be – a very useful warning of stormy weather to come.

Similarly if you look back at the clouds following the passage of a vigorous cold front from west to east you will see them moving rapidly from a southwesterly direction, indicating colder air advancing from the west.

Figures A2.3 to A2.6 show the sequence of weather maps from Chapter 3 with the isotherms and thermal winds superimposed on them. Note how the isotherms are steadily distorted from the almost straight lines of figure A2.3 as cold air moves south behind the cold front and warm air pushes northeast in association with the warm front. As the low develops, the strong westerly winds aloft of figure A2.3 back steadily to southwesterly at the cold front and veer steadily to northwesterly at and ahead of the warm front.

JET STREAMS

The strongest upper level winds are known as jet streams. The title is usually reserved for winds in excess of 80 knots – winds of over 200 knots are not uncommon. They are found where the isotherms are closest together, either along the polar front, or at the warm and cold fronts of a depression (which are distortions of the polar front) at heights between 5000 and 10,000 metres.

Occasionally you may see an almost stationary band of upper cloud – usually altocumulus or cirrocumulus – with the clouds moving rapidly along the line of the band. This is evidence of the jet stream in the position shown in figure A2.3. Subsequent movement of the band will indicate the sort of weather to come. If the cloud edge is advancing with the upper wind well veered from the surface wind, the weather will deteriorate; if the cloud edge is receding with the upper wind backed from the surface wind, the weather will improve.

Figure A2.3

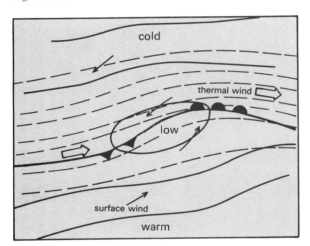

Figure A2.5

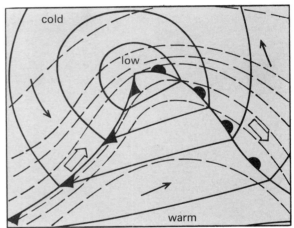

Figure A2.4

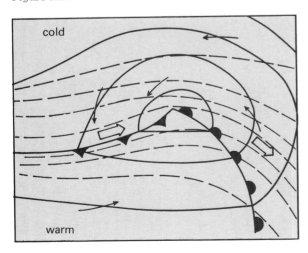

Figure A2.6

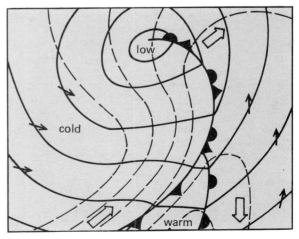

Index to definitions